Original Light

also by ALBERT GOLDBARTH

Ontario Review Press Poetry Series

ORIGINAL LIGHT
New and Selected Poems 1973-1983

Albert Goldbarth

Ontario Review Press
Princeton, New Jersey

Library of Congress Cataloging in Publication Data
Goldbarth, Albert.
  Original light.

  (Ontario Review Press poetry series)
  I. Title.   II. Series.
PS3557.O354O7   1983   811'.54   83-2476
ISBN 0-86538-031-7
ISBN 0-86538-032-5 (pbk.)

Distributed by PERSEA BOOKS, Inc.
225 Lafayette St.
New York, NY 10012

811.54

Notes / Acknowledgements

Original Light chooses from a decade of books; its poems, though, are organized not chronologically but thematically. I'm grateful to my editor Raymond Smith who, working from an early schema of my own, defined this book's three major sections and made all of the final selections for them. Few of these pieces were written with this kind of ordering in mind. They had other concerns, a grimace or a grin, a tilt of breast or the red swipe left by a slap... But I feel, at last, they're at home here.

The "selected" poems come from *Coprolites* (New Rivers Press, 1973), *Jan. 31* (Doubleday, 1974), *Comings Back* (Doubleday, 1976), *Ink Blood Semen* (Bits Press, 1980), *The Smuggler's Handbook* (Chowder Chapbooks, 1980) and *Faith* (New Rivers Press, 1981). Bill Truesdale, Bob Wallace and David Clewell should be singled out here for editorial generosity of a remarkable kind.

I chose not to excerpt from my book-length poems *Opticks* (Seven Woods Press, 1973) and *Different Fleshes* (Hobart & William Smith Colleges Press, 1979); from the chapbook-length poems *Curve* (New Rivers Press, 1977) and *Eurekas* (Raccoon Books / St. Luke's Press, 1981); and from the rather long poems that entirely comprise *Keeping* (Ithaca House, 1975) and *Who Gathered and Whispered Behind Me* (L'Epervier Press, 1981). Nor was it finally practical to include poems from the collections *Under Cover* (The Best Cellar Press, 1972), *A Year of Happy* (North Carolina Review Press, 1976) and *Goldbarth's Book of Occult Phenomena* (Blue Buildings Press, 1982).   .

The pieces that *are* here, "new" and "selected" both, were first published in the following journals, the editors of which are extended my gratitude: *The Agni Review* (A History of Civilization), *The American Poetry Review* (Distances; "On the outskirts of London..."; "In 1856 she won second prize..."), *The Beloit Poetry Journal* (A Sanguinary), *Bits* (Wings), *The Carolina Quarterly* (His Daughter; "Yet Leaving Here a Name..."), *The Chowder Review* (Remembering the Typo), *Crazyhorse* ("And Now Farley Is Going to Sing..."), *The Iowa Review* (Trying; Ssh), *The Minnesota Review* (Witch Trial, Transcript; Dialogues: Winckelmann–Busch; Dialogues: Alkest–Flamel), *The New England Review* (Praise/Complaint; The World of Expectations), *The New Yorker* (And), *The Ontario Review* (M = L/T; All-Nite Donuts; "There is a legend about a piano..."; In Pain; The Accountings; Vacation: an extended postcard; The Form and Function of the Novel), *Poet Lore* ("and in the preface ..."), *Poetry* (The Importance of Artists' Biographies; Worlds; Blue Flowers; Pleasures; A Theory of Wind; Diagrams; Before; The Well), *Poetry Northwest* (Return to the World; Puritania), *Prarie Schooner* (Cross-Country, & Motif Appears), *Salmagundi* (The Harem Boy), *Shenandoah* (The Errors).

A few of these poems were part of a group awarded *Poetry's* Jacob Glatstein Memorial Prize for 1981, and others have been reprinted in the textbook *Writing Poems* (Atlantic-Little, Brown) and the anthology *Night Walks* (Ontario Review Press). As for the time in which some of these pieces were written... two fellowships from the National Endowment for the Arts arrived when they were needed.

Special appreciation to writer-friends John Crisp, Bob Lietz, Carolyn Osborn, Howard Silver, Tony Sobin and Wayne Zade for their continuing warmth and encouragement. Their work at times has made me feel the way they've been good enough to say mine has them. G.B. Edwards' narrator Ebenezer Le Page observes, "I must give it to Clive Holyoak he was a wonderful violin-player. I will never forget the way he used to rise up on his tip-toes on his little short legs to reach the top notes. It wasn't so much as if he was playing the fiddle as if the fiddle was playing him."

*

for Morgan, with original love

CONTENTS

III Chronologues

Original Light

The Importance of Artists' Biographies

*was soon so great that the enduring fame of several [early]
Greek artists—Zeuxis and Apelles, to name but two—rests
on these biographies alone, without there having been any
possibility of later forming an impression of their actual works.*
—Ernst Kris and Otto Kurz

The days go by, then more days go by.
We've all seen a lover from fifty feet, and walked up
to a stranger. Though the stars at fifty
light years are clear. The nights go by,
then more nights go by. We've all leapt on
and in a lover, then fifty minutes later rolled
off a stranger. The air goes farther than eyes go
through it, the days and nights are small
collections on a desktop—matchbooks,
knuckle-sized shells, these opened pages of Kris and Kurz—,
a space takes place
between a life and the attributes of a life,
we've all seen it.

———————

Dürer once painted a spider over
a picture by Michelangelo. And a
good few lucid-looking lovers
of art were duped—the threshold having
been lowered between a life and a credible fiction of life,
by a rod, one causative cone, enough
for an otherwise-discerning aficionado to be going
down the gallery in her floorsweeping silks, her hands
on every picture as if they were fruits to be tested,
as if she does this all of the time and with any drawing,
as if, in a crowd of men from the court,
before Michelangelo's gilt-framed sketch she
hadn't especially tried to squash it.

*

1

And—if Dürer had wholly webbed over
that surface—webbed it to opacity—then
would we know

*

by the broke-nosed, doleful face; the
father's entreaties to turn away from marble, mallets,
mixing-plaques, and the drafty shambles-strewn room;
the nights the Prior allowed him in
with a candle and chalk, to let the flame lick
intermittently up
the legs, the groins, the chest skin now thin as shellac
on the corpses of San Spirito, getting it
down exact; the story of the faked
Sleeping Cupid; the story of the blows with the Pope;
the "great distress of mind and fatigue . . . better
if I had set myself to a cartwright!"; the sonnets,
concerned with absolute beauty opening
like a flower, and the fifteen-year-old boys
he saw as flowers; that, all that, and more, or
just the way the gray veins in his hands' backs
bulged, the only indication of terrible weight, as he rested
his head in the sunstruck floury dust
of the studio, with a mother's gesture of setting her only
child into bed—then

*

would we know to know
the swaths of cloud-borne-glow and
galactic deepnesses, the artisan-like
concentration and bunch-muscled effort of God,
in Michelangelo's charcoal rough
for *Division of Light from Darkness* . . .
would we?

————

Later, in a garden, the courtiers gone back
to the massive halls of power, she'll look at a
real spider doing the business of spiders
among some stems, and idly wonder: what

*

2

it must have been, to be the first man—or
maybe she'll think it as woman—to see, to really see,
this creature as itself: a black-backed
stalk-eyed sac-bellied pinch-jawed scuttler on too
many too bristled legs. *And would I know,*
from that, the nubbin inside
that lets out length after length of this delicate
engineering, this stuff
a bug-gland's-weight away from being pure
filamented sun . . .

*

She may not be a lady of the court
come from parrots and cakes, but
my lover
I lifted, I differed away
from any ready semblance, then set down

*

here, on a page, in my study. I recognize
her, though. And you might too if you knew her.
Up in a corner, a spider's spinning this
real web that enters your world
as a word, "web," on a page, "this" page, then
light through a window
lifts the spider as light lifts everything
seeable and brings it, at the same speed
it was just now brought to my eyes,
to the stars.

———————

Science fiction is full of these distances.
Quasar travel. Planet hops.
As if a time warp were stranger than time.
The days go by, then more days go by.
Often the world is hollow; a central, a generating,
civilization lives in the shell. These books surmise
its whip wars with The Lizard Tribe and The Worm,
its celestial ballet when the wings are in season,

the sprigs above its parturition doors, its blood dance,
even the simple distilling of lavender and citron
out of the air at night, by the shore of its inner sea ...
surmise all this by looking at life
as we know it, our own long neighborhood blocks,
the secrets in laundromats' spins and urgent impressions
on notepads left by the phone—as if a man
could walk this city we live in, stop still at the corner of
Zeuxis and Apelles, think deep, and put some law
of inference to work. For him, the Earth might be a
kind of conceptual crystal, and what we call our
autobiographies would only be refractions of some
original light at the core. We've all had the feeling
he's right. The nights go by, then more nights go by.
We've all seen the faces of lovers in sleep
go somewhere, maybe back to their source, and we
lay by the breathing of strangers. We've all seen
the faces return. I couldn't guess the distance between
a word I write and your reception of it, astronomy
hasn't such measure. But everybody's walked
above the bones of the mothers, the bones of the fathers,
the grandparent bones going back to the magma
heart of it all, through dragon bones, the flightbones
of a pegasus, the first fine organization of grains
of bone in a luminous nucleus ... There are spaces
so vast, words fail, light fails, though maybe the crossing
is only from a day to another day.

———————

And if the blue look that came over Zeuxis
after one rough *kylix* too many of that white wine
he washed down the mussels with

                        meant his

taking the spiral frieze off
that last *kylix*, as the model for his own gold
opulent coruscations of fruit trees

                        we'll

never know, will we, we'll never really know.

*

4

In my study, I come close. There's a print
by Saul Steinberg: a desk, and the objects of its
arrangement: a ruler, a spool of gray thread,
a box of matches, an austere shell with only
the slightest blush of vulva-pink inside it,
a sketchbook opened casually to a nuthatch
done from a pencil's bold strokes, the pencil...
                         *
I take off my glasses, stare at that wall,
I come as close as I can. The desktop
fades to almost never having been.
                         *
And out of the blurred hints left, I see
as I've seen up there impossibly for years:
an old man on an old burro,
heading heavily toward the right margin.
For years now, heading away
in their own shape, from the shapes of Steinberg's
placing.
          It's raining. The old man is
violet, and soft—the kinds of small shadows
worn flannel casts. The burro is weary. It isn't
giving up, though. They're carrying something
—the small tools of a life. Perhaps he's a peddler,
and this is his work, that comes out of
the work of others.

_____

A spider remains in a corner through all of this,
a lover remains in my bed. The night,
the sightless webbed-over night, goes by,
then it's day. It happens that way.
The sketchbook in my Steinberg print is fixed
to a page marked "nuthatch," fixed unturnably,
though it's day, then it's night, and in a way
time turns that world as I can turn pages
in Kris and Kurz...
               An asterisk calls
attention elsewhere. So this is the shape

of a spider, that I've taken off a "real" wall
for this "wall," on this page. It's morning.
A lady I know is still asleep. Light lifts a spider.
Light lifts the lady, and lifts me, though I never move,
and light lifts a spider. The birth of our sun
is first being seen on other planets, a flash
some registerial hand beyond
our understanding duly records. A spider is one
continuous tunnel of being a spider, as long
as light is long, as far; and if the cosmos
curves, a spider returns, at least
a picture of spider returns—as we return, merely
by the saying of that, to Dürer. For him,
it's another morning. He adds one last
perfectionist's dab to the little wiseass joke he's played
in a square inch of Michelangelo. He looks up
now, confused for a moment, confused and exalted,
as if...There are times when we're sensitized to it...
The whole air around him is pictures,
the light is a gallery. Nothing, he sees, can be lost.

I
Distances

$$M = \frac{L}{T}$$

Moths he writes me *gourmandized the Virgin*
of blue brocade, with ruby, broccoli-brown and ocher, off
the study wall. They'd grazed her like cows
at clover. Prophylacticism,
recompense and penance all require, first, imaginable
damage—what religious law foresaw this pick-clean
desecratory eating? Or this: an infant's popping
the holy gold bar of *mezuzah* off the rabbi's table straight

in its mouth, and irretrievably down from there like any
foilwrapped sweetmeat. This was southern France, the only
village synagogue for counties about, and its only
gold bar of *mezuzah*. Every blackhat, sidelock *Hassid*
blanched—the baby burped—the sacred scroll in the gold bar
of *mezuzah* settled down for the night in more secular
scrollwork: bowel. Well I've snacked strange things
too, at Grasse and Cannes: snout salad,

once; and once a lady out of her foggy Sorbonne undies
left a taste on my tongue as new as did the carts
the vendors opened redolently up each dawn when sun
threw off its own fog; then the patties
of unpasteurized cheeses, little tied teepees of leeks,
and fresh-skinned hares hung by the hindlegs
so gravity still pulled commas of blood from their noses
onto the flat white wrapping paper: said something

to the body almost beatific in power. I
can close my eyes and taste her yet. Memory, individual
or collective, means this formula for Lasting
over Travel. I've seen hundreds kneel hundreds of hard years
after the fact, if it was a fact: at the Shrine
of the Virgin of Guadalupe, under that cactus-fibre shawl She out
of nowhere appeared on. Hundreds—kneeled like a flock, in their own
way grazing her—and so I thought of his letter. Miracle's

just that: memory lasting over impossible travel. In
Texas, lakewater, mineral-green, throws and throws
its white lace at the land—its foam a
peek of slip—and I think of the darkgarbed grandmamas in rhythm
smacking the laundry rock that summer in France; or of
the many negligees the many women tossed in many corners
before I settled with you—and that you've loved me over
so long a lean time now, I think qualifies

as miracle, by which I mean dramatic, odds-defying
comings through. The infant wasn't hurt. The stool
was stirred and the gold with its Word found whole.
Then I looked heavenward, actually ceilingward, and there
were huge coccoons by the hundred, ruby and blue, as
true as the silk they were supped from. She was meant
to be delivered by wings. *I tell you they*
reformed the Virgin! I almost believe it. I want to

believe it: *perfect, down to Her bodice's lace.*

Worlds

1120's not only the year Eirik Gnupson
—or in some accounts Upsin—"sailed
in search of Vinland," but the time
you left. In Europe the world was still

damn flat. A map: a kind of earth-tone plane with
blue braiding over the sides. I know
because at the most hurt moment, my hands
were also stuck halfway through an explanation,

just like the watch's, too
run down for further time, and it was 11:20
forever. It works by accident
placing an object—a pine cone primed

to be lobbed by treesex, a cheese-smudged knife blade, really
anything—at the center of ultimate damage
or engendering, and that's its symbol
irrevocably: for me, your leaving

is always a watchface
held halted in its own two hands. In
the forested lands of the first Norse visits,
the sign of a new world

happening, every day, was maybe
a pine chest made ornate by a border of cones,
or a knife fresh out of the cheese with
American light (before

its naming) glimmering the little
naked metal left. And so, by some signs, two
worlds overlap, as any moment is a point
in the depth of chronology as

11

well as some fractioned degree of a time zone
set in a linear surface. This morning
a woman with nape-length cornsilk hair
was leaning a jamb in a pose just this

side of crumpled, and running her hair ends
through her lips, again and again, for the simple
comforts of touch and repetition. Maybe,
I thought, she's thinking of love's two enemies: distance,

proximity. She made me think of you. She
made me see, as if through seahaze, someone
angled in a cabin door
near the piles of timber and fox fur, picking

idly at her Viking braid, again and again, in a
sisterhood of body-slump and heart's-thump
simultaneity claims for itself, outside of
what we call calendar years. Imagine

an antique map, its edging of monsters. Back
then you'd just fall off. —From a line or a globe, the
pain's the same. Back then they didn't have
watches to stop and so their world did.

Blue Flowers

. . . do tend to be associated with colder
climates and greater heights.
—Bronowski

Autumn. Light's the world's list.
Over breakfast I think of Linnaeus
over a taxidermied ocelot body,
a perfect dragonfly under a perfect
tag, a turbot, a marmoset.
The dragonfly already less bright than the

pins of its systemization. And
by lunch we're at it still, "Remember
the knowing shameful tilt of about
10° you give your head when avoiding all
responsibility," the lucid, detailed, inarguable,
relentless cataloguing

of how it works and doesn't, every
interlocking, every glandular turbine,
the sexual ratchets, thinking's various honeys,
the day shift in the marrow. This
is clarity: assignatory, pure.
Outside, the day accumulates

itself: tree, hosiery, bannister, skin
on skin. A domino at the window: momma
squirrel again, dark teats on buff belly. I
see him in the high, attentive air
of Lapland, 1745, compiling his final
tables, breathing on his hands and naming

absolutely, naming it all, no matter.
Flower in the fields of the flawed
—wild harelip. Brilliant bloom
in the meadows of excellence—diamondcutter's-blow.
Then dinner, then dark. To walk
our late November streets without slipping go

13

of this strict ticking-off of minutiae, not
yet, no not while the severest sliver of light
lets our lives be our subjects—is to breathe out
pale blue blossoms, the only kind left. Exact,
exacting beauty—the words above which
only lichen lives, and above that only the stars.

Distances

and closenesses, and the line between. Three inches
of earth might pack time from the trilobite
to the first clean Jericho kilnwork . . .
Here's a man, in a tower. It's dark and
once a day they give him bread and clotted milk.
He *thinks* it's once a day—the dark is
unrelieved by notions like "night" or "morning."
He thinks it's been ten years. He scratches
stickmen on the stones, and tells them stories
of a world called Out. He's in. The stone is
three inches thick—not much, unless it's everything.

*

What I didn't understand about light was
stars. Their light hit Earth—that was a
condition of "star," as 8th-grade science had it.
There were hundreds of thousands—Mr. Andrews
pulled down a chart, and there were hundreds of thousands
of bodies up there, hurtling light at Earth . . .
Then why was outer space so dark? What
happened? I think that man in the tower
must be in such light, as we are
when we sleep—and everything shining travels
a space so strange we don't see it.

*

If it's true of hundreds of thousands of bodies it's
true of one. I think that I'm a carrying-case
for something—because it's dark inside, because
there are these breathing-holes over the surface . . .
I guess I'm talking about the mind. It sleeps around.
It spends a third of its time unfaithful
to the body. They didn't explain it in 8th-grade science
that way, but sometimes I think of consciousness

15

and flesh as two lovers, asleep. You know that
truth about bodies: their asses touching, their
backs to each other, their faces in separate directions.

*

It was 8th grade that I fell for Janice Netter, I
could take my place three inches from her in gym line and
it might as well have been all of archeology's
wafery layering intervening...Then Mr. Andrews
would talk about light, in a prism, and this
became an initial lesson in distance's subjectivity.
Say they finally arrive, from Out. They want to give him
a home with windows again, lovers, roasted goose.
It's been ten years. He clings to a stone and growls.
He doesn't want to leave his stickmen,
those he feels closest to.

A History of Civilization

In the dating bar, the potted ferns lean down
conspiratorially, little spore-studded
elopement ladders. The two top buttons
of every silk blouse have already half-undone all
introduction. Slices of smile, slices of sweet brie,
dark and its many white wedges. In back

of the bar, the last one-family grocer's is necklaced
over and over: strings of leeks, greek olives, sardines.
The scoops stand at attention in the millet barrel,
the cordovan sheen of the coffee barrel, the kidney beans.
And a woman whose pride is a clean linen apron polishes
a register as intricate as a Sicilian shrine. In back

of the grocery, dozing and waking in fitful starts
by the guttering hearth, a ring of somber-gabardined grandpas
plays dominoes. Their stubble picks up the flicker like filaments
still waiting for the bulb or the phone to be invented. Even their
coughs, their phlegms, are in an older language. They move the simple
pieces of matching numbers. In back

of the back room, in the unlit lengths of storage, it's
that season: a cat eyes a cat. The sacks and baskets
are sprayed with the sign of a cat's having eyed a cat, and
everything to do with rut and estrus comes down to a few
sure moves. The dust motes drift, the continents.
In the fern bar a hand tries a knee, as if unplanned.

All-Nite Donuts

A customer's blowing
smoke rings almost

heavy as the dough o's rising
out of the vat of grease.

Outside, the whores are whistling
their one note, lips thick

donuts strawberry-glazed.
Inside, the register will open its drawer

for a quarter and make its single cheep.
At midnight I thought it

ugly, all these lime and lavender
stools along the counter like a used

car salesman's breath mints.
Maybe it is. But somehow now, by

three, the special bloodshot view
of overdue eyes finds special beauty

in this neon and its attendant fly,
both fitfully buzzing. —Not a classic beauty,

no, the whores don't swivel slightly
toward a passing trick like flowers

toward the sun, it isn't a bit like that.
But all of our zeroes are here

made sweet. I dunk one in a mug,
I raise decaffeinated instant in a toast

to what's available, when we need it,
all night. Some guy goes by. The whores

curve slightly, like plastic spoons
being worked in a hardening cheese dip.

Pleasures

The view from the dungeon's barred slit is
a tree. It's fall. Another leaf swirls down,
exactly fits its shadow. And a prisoner
alone with a wall understands how his days
too are a kind of shadowboxing in which the
shadow wins. Not far away really,

the Emperor lifts a plum by silver plum tongs.
From his shoulder, a mechanical bird,
a lark, is singing—its garnet-and-emerald
throat by his ear like a barber's clippers humming
the wish to fly. Its eyes are onyx. A woman
and a milk bath in the chalcedony tub is

just the thing after plums! The mechanical
woman, today. Its parts are a purring
in honey. And, like a bottle of fine wine, it's
best kept on its back. The faucets
are the antlers of a golden deer whose golden rider,
a woods nymph, pours appropriately from her cold

and hot nipples. She holds a gold tray for the soaps.
Some mornings, real deer enter the grounds. The
Emperor feeds them apples the scullery-domo
sixteenths, and their breaths against his palm
are heavier and grainier than the fruit. So
many pleasures! The deer, so delicate!—though

they appear in poems with tiresome regularity:
their tremulous sides, their elegant bamboo gait,
etc. Why not more of the beveled isinglass
stare of this handtooled copper doe with the
musicworks inside? Or toasters! How
about a plane of morning light being fixed

in an oblong on the mirrory side of a toaster!
Even now, somebody's wavery face
in such a composition may be eloquent of what
survives past pain—and it floats,
on silver, like the exhalations of kneeling
deer one autumn, like unconscious prayer. How

about it? So many pleasures! Even
the loud smear of tripe being hosed down a gray
market gutter, even the small white bird
of milk on a child's upper lip, umbrella's
metal spider, crazy lace of blood in the eyelid,
labyrinth gnat-belly, flamesnap, darkness,

waking in darkness, being yourself in darkness through
despondency, even a man about to place his head
in his hands and he sees, against them, yes how his
face exactly fits its shadow. Now it's fall, and so
chill, and his life is something he can still hold and
rub his face in, real, and warm, and nubbled lovely.

The Errors

Central YMCA Community College, Chicago

1.
When your sad the whole world seams wrong.

You've raised your hands like treasure divers surfacing from the gray
bends of the brain with pearls
of miscomprehension, so many breast-pins engraved
with wrong dates. But I want to show you something: these
are the hands that nuzzled a woman's photo and now she wears
his thumbprint for her face; this, the thumb
sucked as if a man would hitch
toward infancy—thumbs
opposed the fingers, invented hammers, built, his
contributed tool was the wrecking-ball
socketed to his wrist; and her birthday poem, the light typed touch
that could have quieted trembling: in these hands *subtle* warped
to *bustle* till the years fell. And now I place them,
palms up, wrong
five-legged beasts with their underbellies exposed, on the desk
for you who have told me, in your own broken wedding
of English and your birthtongue, how *the U.S. sends tanks
and your welcome, how the baby hasd no father so
her fren gots a hanger give her a abortcher*—I
know, I grade your papers, the difference between the alphabet
and inkstains leaks from your pens every day thin
as thought. And these, my own
botched lines, the ones in the palmistry handbook
under *Incorrigible*, ask for grading too. So I give them
to you, tonight, the poem
for the Spanish chick who wrote about her first two weeks
in America: a rape on the bus and the driver's La Brea-black adam's apple
spit on a knife, said they'd also scooped her purse, said the landlord
opened her one trunk of clothes to the rain. We laughed.
Said she'd come on an errplane.

2.
An adult does have controll of the lifes of young people to a certain extinct.

So we whimper, and our buttocks whipped
by their own blue nerves; how efficient, penitents born with congenital
lash. And this is the self-inflicted confession, or its next step,
expiation: I've been wrong
with you, as a lit window too high up
can be wrong and the flocks mistake something that thin, glass,
for dimension. Often you thought this pleased me, these dead birds, but
that was no pillow. And for whole nights there has been no place
for my head. If, then, in my sleeplessness, I mocked your sentences,
awkward, and never to take flight, the laughable
dodos in the evolution of prose, you'll forgive my forgetting what
those constructs meant to you, or your pointing out the *pengwin*
& orstirch don't fly neither Mr. Goldbart but could beat
your God Damm lark to a pulp. And you've
been wrong with me. This expectation, that I would clone myself
whole in the lives of each of you . . . In the cliché "thirst for knowledge" I
was the reservoir you would faucet at whim. Why is that a too
cute metaphor? What's a cliché? You, the girl in the back
I thought of eleven lines above at the mention of *nights*, and *pillow*,
aren't you listening? Isn't now the time for real
colloquy, here: and I'm beginning with this, my own list of tics
and overexposures, and now it's your turn. For I've seen the hound's teeth
working in the gosling's throat, and an infant whose asshole was given
to thalidomide and it shit out its mouth . . . and what we think
are errors: belong, and repeat, motifs we wake in the night and
sweat at. And if I invited you over? here, to my house, for the last class,
and we swept glass fragments up from around the old, avian
misdirection, and strung them for necklaces. Oh, sure, there's rich
perfect glass: that's lucidity. But here, these chips of cheap sheeting of ours:
how the light, when we tilt right, goes rainbow in the flaws.

23

3.
The tasted of it is to enjoy flesh smell fluit.

A friend writes: KAYAK took his poem, and printed the line "thin dresses"
tin dresses, says "my surrealist affiliations only go
so far." I counter with BACK DOOR's prestidigitating my "rabbi"
rabbit. We could war all day, lugging ever larger pyramids of typos
to our howitzers, and never lose the joy of computing injustices. Yes, there are
wrongs, miscalculations, for weeping; 'natch: such deprivations
as the insomniac's dream, the mermaid's hymen; even now, the small print
in the litigation harbors such malevolences as could raze a house's foundations
with their pincers; even now, aren't I the man
who tried to dance in the space between the grains
of a pour of salt; the husband in the coffin doesn't blink,
it's the widow's blurring of vision; that's no silver spoon
in the newborn mouth, it's his eyes spilling silver nitrate...But
I've lived errors that, like synesthesia—flesh fruit—, are fortuitous
mismatching and, in the burst breath of a spoonerism, *crime of passion* calmed
to *prime of caution*, and we all survived. An error is: nails sleeping on a bed
of man—but some have made a religion of that
reversal, daily walk in Jesus' grace. There are insides-out
illuminating our waking, worlds where milk's skimmed off
the top and the bucket of cream gleams like ivory. My friend
M., result of a pin-riddled rubber; my parents, together
26 years from the day they blundered one inch in
each other at Humboldt Park Lagoon; there are accidents
we bless, there are rabbits ordained to bless them, and some
couplings unsymmetrical as a-man-and-a-woman we call
love and writhe with the lack of. It's that
kind of error I wish you, my students, my timid women lifting
suds-white ankles out of tin dresses, my composition assignment, a guy
says Columbus opened up a whole new world. For trade. Says
he set sail for the undies.

4.
Being togeter with you are woundefill.

Columbus wakes, with incisive, atlantic, tears in his eyes: *wrong
wrong, no Cathay!* Don't cry, Christopho. I'm here, New
York, writing this and reading Glyn Daniel's *Prehistory*, let us be yours
in vindication. He tales how a hare breaks
for cover, the hound follows baying into the lost labyrinthine passages
under the Dordogne hills, and when he's finally retrieved
by the ears up a fault in rock, four schoolboys have bumbled
onto the leaping russet cows of Lascaux. Felicitous wrong
turn. There are errors to let the light in, listen: earlier someone
goofed—errplane—and we laughed, a student wrote once how
they laufed at me, so hard, they were in statues. I think
his word misuse is true—the stiffening, muffling
effects of derision. Combating that, "the prehistorian
witnesses how it is cutlery *sherds* and statuary *fragments*, the
mishaps of daily making-do, that endure
when even philosophy, say, or linguistics perish. The noblest cultures
shape themselves about the remains of their rubbish chutes." The breakage
that tells. The history of our worlds, written
in erasure. Isn't this the one thing
we, all, want to learn: that mistake between us
so breakable, if ever it cracks we'll be married as true
as a kidney transplant—perfect hugging forever...Now class
come pillowed around my table, the final exam
tonight is to butcher good taste,
and sentences. Let's try. Let's trust
in our fuckups—that rich, embarrassing trove, and let's
say, *really say*, something indestructible out of groan and clamor,
and we will meat for a hurt
to hurt talk, and with our cleaverest words
eschew the fat.

Remembering the Typo

New moon—no
more than a pocketwatch with
just a gleam of the case showing.

I give up. Why *do* large corporations
assume time has something to do with the hands
of a clock—like a cop's
directing traffic? No wonder
their roofs blow whistles.

Once, I wrote about driving Iowa,
60 m.p.h.: "The fields
blend like tempera." I believe
the opal, the ovum, the crystal stretch
of spit in a cat's yawn, schist-glint,
blood-thump, hotel
in the nautilus, I believe

the celery's strings
compacted into their white-green
vegetable body like a harp
the eons are pressuring toward a diamond...

are the mechanisms,
surer than jewels, that
real time is run by. It was celery

batter-fried in a Japanese restaurant,
so reminded me, and I told my friends about
the typo: "The fields blend like tempura."
I believe that in the space
between those two letters, a kind of time
takes place in which a dream's understanding

of estrus, starfire,
death's imperious ticking, and

how air sleeps around
(sweet tramp, so often tasting
of strangers' bodies)...

I say, a kind of time takes place
in which a dream's understanding
flies like an owl, hungers,
hunts and fucks, though it
snores through the rational
light of the work day.

Pulling this string
of celery out of my teeth may even
start it up, may be
initiating the gears. I mean
the big time, I mean the only time,
the time when a wind is feeling me,

feeling me, saying
this one isn't ripe yet
but one day.

A Theory of Wind

This is how the page must feel: it doesn't
understand God. Whatever the language
on that page, an Eastern script as fine
as dendrite, or the harsh Germanic squatting
of black retrievers at obedience school, or
even the floating eye and spiked sun
of pictographs, that language
has a saying for God's inscrutable ways.
I mean a woman is wailing and there's
nothing the shaman can do. I mean

it's night. The wind at my body is wild
animals licking for salt. I've set a
sheet of galleys down and come outside for these
rough tongues! The wind in the monstrous condor
flappings of my banana tree leaves,
the wind in the twiddling back grasses.
No ant egg is free.
Everywhere, objective and efficient:
its assessment. No wonder tribal life thought
God behind such touch. It deepens,

mnemonic, my own taking stock
of the night: a slippery siamese-conjoining
where two cars' oil drippings braid at the curb;
these separate orange lips
of fungus making the rotten log a portraitist's
doodling; every follicle in catflesh, and its
millipartite contributing toward a perfect arch...
It *is* perfect, all of it, each burr an asterisk
calling attention to limitless exactitude. Even the
word *burr*, how it—click!—fits. But

the wind is indifferent to this. Out of a window
a long cry, *why*, and again, *why*, *why*, whatever
the reason, is saying something of how an oak

goes down in gale force, a marble column is
found in pieces, breezes lick another inch of forest
fire along the green floor...it was *burn*, not
burr. Just when we write it: perfectly wrought,
the typesetter reads it: perfectly wrong. And then
the long hours correcting. If it's true for this
level it's true for that level, but anyway no shaman

or oncologist explains it. *Why?* The wind
is come chill through her room tonight. *Why?* And what
was my page supposed to say? Our lively lust,
list?, last?, our lovely dust...it's so hard
to remember. It's always night, somewhere.
Some tree is always unsafe. And all we can do
is pray for ours, in our backyard, that we thought
so pure of form, its bark moire like Persian lamb...
but what do we know? The wind is going over
everything tonight, proofing for error.

**"There is a legend about a piano
that somehow got flushed into the sewers of Chicago."**
—Lawrence Wright

Light even more than water seemed inviolate
to him, more a state than a thing, a field
no action or object on entering could
really disrupt. It diminished but never broke.
While dark—and here he entered the mildew-perfumed
sacristy, and bumped on an upturned altar—
could be pierced, by light...By now
he's through the chancel, where in fact the light's
so whole it lifts you into it, and we'll never know
the rest of St. Augustine's optics
metaphysics. This is the moment as recorded
in his *Confessions* when he chances on his mentor
St. Ambrose bent to the poundage
of thick fifth-century pages, each one starting
with a letter like a trumpeteer in livery, and each one
bordered in birds as perfectly folded
as a child's prayer—St. Ambrose "reading

without moving his lips." The very mention
means shock. Of course—the understanding of script
was in transition. It's that moment in time,
in Milan, while real birds
outside let real song into the light
until it's part of the light, and shit their chiaroscuro
on the black sills, and preen, and loverub...But
Augustine, trained as an orator, he
for whom the language was a spoken art; and writing,
a score: as for music—Augustine
gawks at Ambrose reading purely mentally, and the
world he's sure of wobbles. It's a lovely
vignette, profounder than its author
ever knew. I think it's lovely too, to look through
one of those black-silled windows and freeze-frame

Augustine reading: what it meant: a single word
the lips gave meaning to, with some of the comprehending,
leisure and intimacy
of artisans' hands chasing gold leaf, sanding wood.
A word must have been like a lover's nipple, let
go only when tasted completely and
fully peaked. Now say that sentence
out loud, from your body, one eked sound at a time
and with deliberation. This is how it was,

that piano, how it had to have been: each key of it
dropped discretely down the flush: a most partite

glissando. I remembered that legend
as Carla played a Mozart sonata, her face
no longer really in the room but
someplace higher. There are things we need to believe
about our lives: that days accumulate
toward something greater than days, and that
a pattern exists so even the hammerblows, maybe
only the hammerblows, admit
an exaltation. This is what Carla said,
this is what Carla said with her striking. Her
eyes were closed. The room like a number had
timesed itself, with music. My eyes were closed
and behind them I saw someone

in Chicago, tired of tinkling his tinpan-alley ivories
barside every night, follow all of those individual keys
with their strings, and every string
according to its placement in the hierarchy of scale
made its own quick arabesque
in the water, swirled, and then was
sucked irretrievably down to where
workers process our large commonality: tampon
applicators, rubbers milky like snakeslough, home
abortions, letters hot as fire but torn to snow,
dead pets, live hurts, and of course the worldwide,

equalizing, seedbearing, rich mucks of riddance.
How those keys and strings assembled
again, if they did and the legend says they did,
I can't describe exactly—it's a mystical business
and has to do with this very idea

of what we share, the basics, and their
ultimate uniting. If it took place in the sewers, still
there was little in its difference from that other mystical
Oneness, St. Augustine's light: that holds,
and timeses ourselves, and is never less than entire.
When he reads, it's the earliest rosary; a word: a bead
in a long string. Abnegation
is his instrument, and he improvises with passion.
I-de-ny, his concert goes, *de-ny*, *de-ny*. Beatitude
begins with refusal. Remember, it's 400 years
before the Church allowed organ music.
It's 1400 years before the Florentine Bartolomeo

Cristoforo produced the first piano. Today
even priests get to do a little
boogie-woogie jamming. Carla plays, and ears
are on their knees in a secular reverence. But
I want to focus on stone in the sun
of the early fifth century: Augustine
at the latrine. Though that's a mighty word
for this meager and straightforward
runnel cut in rock. For us it's porcelain.
For him it's this plain catching of his
plain arc. The sun has traveled hundreds of
thousands of miles to be the amber backdrop for this
amber act. And he's so unimaginably far

from us, he once saw an angel, really saw an angel,
standing on the beach. At his mentor
Ambrose's birth, "some bees swarmed on his mouth,"
and this was prophecy of a life of sweet speech.
And Ambrose saw an angel. And Ambrose
fell in a trance to see St. Martin die 500 miles

away in Tours. And Ambrose discovered the buried
bodies of giant twins. Those times were different,
except when they were the same. Now Augustine
holds his cloak to a side,
the great gold string plays out, and
—though there's no piano for centuries yet—
like anyone's, it tinkles.

Trying

That night, he had a vision. He was
in Heaven. The ground was a field
of flowers, unending in duration
and beauty both; even the fleshy orchids,
even the tulips' flambeaux: were sized
to queen anne's lace and baby's breath,
evenly as teeth. Everyone flew. The wings
were simple, like hands of cards
of down, but efficacious. No more
preparation, huff or flex or long upgathering,
than the casual shrugging
off of Earth a wood dove shows: and
whole congregations performed their
alleluiahs by the easy dip and rise
of the wren or the swallowtail. And,
like birds, they'd marry
in the air. The women moved their bodies
in and out with the smoothness
and music of concertinas. The men were
hard-buttocked. Legs opened lazily
overhead and made circles for hours
like ceiling fans. Sometimes, at night, what
seemed a kind of atmospheric
energy gathered around somebody's skull, then
crackled in great charged
worms of light, and somebody
else perhaps a mile off would lean
like a typesetter's slant-mark in the sky
and softly go, Ah. So this was
thinking in Heaven. The only sign
of what he supposed to be age was a kind of
accumulated grace, a swan's
or diamond cutter's, in certain
turns of neck and wrist. The food was just
there, on shelves of leaves, as were reed-plaited
kits of pen nibs, bits of wire, yarn, penny nails.

But these went mostly untouched. There was
no need; and no effort. Nobody tried,
though he may have watched days. The weather,
always, was blank-paper perfect. And he woke

weeping, with a shiver even
December air couldn't cause, and paced
the stained oak floor he'd laid himself,
paced maybe an hour, until the morning
fully filled its first thin skin
of light, and his gristmill
circling had ground the fear down.
He'd need to get moving. He cracked
the ice in the porcelain wash-basin,
splashed the last of it off. The
basin and matching pitcher, flower
decorated: tiny intricate blooms a
British ceramicist
set regularly on the surfaces, beautiful, almost
the small near-uniform dots
of a tabloid photograph
forming, for the proper distance, a
well-snapped scene: some tinkerer
straining a biplane together, some
sleepless shlep over something just this
side of a workable phonograph: news
from the music world, from the flying.
Trying.

Return to the World

There's darkness; then there's an opalescent web
on the darkness, lax then taut...

If only it were as easy for you as
for astronauts; for deepsea divers.

Under it all, and undulant, a man
will have to rise from the level

of hundredsucker worms, the globular
comb jellies hanging like japanese lanterns,

stars with fins, stars with teeth,
the tube-eyes, the blind-eyes, cucumbers and moons,

will have to rise then rest
before the final break to air, while blood

remembers its birth barometrics
on land, takes a breath, and accommodates.

Or somebody back from the weightless
spaces beyond direction, beyond the idea of volume

having contents, somebody splashed
down, bound from the capsule at last,

will bide time in re-entry, sorting his nearerness
to other suns' lights out of our light.

At least they have a story to tell,
a rock. I touched one, at the National

Aeronautics and Space Museum. But
you ... There in the final fading

of a dream, before the morning clears
that fog from out of the bramble-thicket

the thinklines in your brain are; or
in illness's last thin sweat... Already

you don't remember. If only you
could also return to this world

with your knowledge intact:
There is a life around our lives for which we're gills.

The nova and ovary, yes, are sisters.
The lungs are small bundles of sky.

Still Lives

What is it about this draped arrangement of green batiste
with Chinese oranges glowing like coals in its folds.
This grapefruit open for business: a pink motel
of tissuey rooms. These plums looking dusted with talcum.
In the long sad line of egg and avocado leading
up to the dented tureen, what is it that tells us they'll
be made to suffer the singing of hymns before supper.
What is it. This spoon that holds the whole blue ceiling
but says a story of emptiness. The way that sack of kittens
caught in stasis becomes a potato. The way a potato leans
outside of its own deep-umber definition, into
the hump of another potato, which is shaded
off into haze. The sharing of confidences. The calling
of body to body, two lute squashes hung as if
in facing pawn shop windows. This peony.
This vase. That bug-eyed bass with just a comma
of its entrail juices, as clear as springwater. What
is it about them. What is it about the sweet
accumulation of meat, of wedge of meat
on wedge, in the rooms of the grapefruit hotel.
What is it about the dented moon
in the chill of the dented tureen—we know
by inference she's working tonight, she's pulling the seas
and the crazy high blood of wolverines, she's earning
so her husband the sun, the great Talmudic scholar,
can spend his days in the study of glory.
What is it. What is it ever. There's a dirty glove that requires a step
away to be a mallard. And a group of bings is tilted
as if waiting for the duck's enormous limp body to be placed
in the stars. The bings, the near-black, clear, fat
caviar of a tree. The chilies. The cocoa beans.
What is it about this lustreware ladle of dijon mustard
folding the light so it looks like Van Gogh's ear.
It's near the little apple knife, it's frightening.
Or is that tiny silver blade by the delicate spirals of appleskin
a sardine. What is it. This is the light from inside

a pearl, and it's hard to tell. This is the border
where radishes meet, the small red dwarves, the long
arthritic blacks, and talk like second cousins
with different languages, talk beyond translation.
What is it. The cheap ceramic kettle with chartreuse willows
on its round side bended back by an invisible wind, so
giving the kettle the look of motion, giving the thick, the almost
spongy, steam the look of a railroad engine's flag of speed.
The leeks. The ewer. The rum. There is a legend
of a saviour appearing in days of mighty travail, that must be
what the ample-buttocked burgher pears are congregated to buzz
about, such is their obvious gravity and intimate
disposition in a corner of silk with dove-and-tulip borders.
That must be. And if it's not, it must be the symbol of it,
for us, for someone. The suck-button arm of a squid. Its
curve as eloquent as an architect's stencil, at least.
Its slippery texture, its length. Its horizontal run in front
of the spherical singlemindedness of grapes, and what that means
of apposition and love. What does it mean. What is it.
The grapes are green. The other grapes are a purple only known
in the bellies of certain dragonflies and shellfish, and an outer
constellation of them lightens into the pure emphatic
red of a borscht. What this does to the green grapes. What
does it do. This sprig of mint. That garlic. What is it.
That Spanish onion, peeling its purple
flophouse wallpaper of a face. These lovely kidney beans, the insides
of our bodies must look like this in their dreams. The jazzy
juiced drupes of the blackberries, of the raspberries, and the bland
sweep of a crockery cup of cream—it's newly risen
to the top and gleams as tough as an ivory pendant.
Yams. A single, languid, yellow rose. The thoughtful intervention
of a yellow rose amid a uniformed squadron of yams.
What is it about disparity, about whatever binds.
How many medals for valor and savagery might be
these beads of water on an eggplant, with the nickels
of light at their centers. The milkweed
choir in its golden bottle, white-robed, unperturbed
by anything fleshly. And the sexual enthusiasm of one
buff, blush-bodied peach for another, for anything,

their velvet clefts, the single hour the clock
of a grapefruit-half counts off, the cheap rooms and the sixty
sweet pink minutes. Yes, and of course the censorious
pointing of a celery. Why, and what of it. These assumings
of our attributes, this easy way of saying the egalitarian
meetings of bananas, the smooth crude blueprint of a human hand
that's a true-drawn bunch of ripening bananas,
what is it. This is any artichoke
in absolute cross-section, with its heart like a cast-bronze
Buddhist god in its temple niche, its heart like a dancing
green flame god! This is the candle; this,
the gelid slab of hogfat just gradations away from
being a candle. This is their agreement, in a special color
shared by them, a wonderful waxy pastel. What
is it. Let me introduce the tomatoes, some done as
if early, with patches of yellow like an infant's soft spot
making you want to weep for what you were. And so
they're on the sill. The grain of the sill. The exact
crack in the plaster. What is it about. The breast of flour.
The cruet. A peppermill. The impossible commune of corn.
An orchid. What is it about an orchid. Why can't I say
I see these things in them. The calling of like. The anther
and the radio. What is it about
the spill of milk brushed blue and gray and it's white
against the hickory, the lean-to and the spire
and the temple column of simple carrots simply placed, the parsley's
green mantilla of lace, the tongs, the towels, the smallest
of the rumples in a towel, the poem of the heel of bread,
of pigtrotter and of brie, and of swiss, and of veins in the blue,
of wheat like a rain,
of salt like a snow
of enormous hard
cartons of weeping.

"And Now Farley Is Going to Sing
While I Drink a Glass of Water!"

At the Vent Haven Museum in Fort Mitchell,
Kentucky, over 500 wooden
ventriloquist's dummies sit
in lit approximations of interrelationship,
stand in small posed groups no stiffer
than friends in half of the photos you own,
grotesque, exaggerated in overblown grimace
or underdefined like a slug, and some equipped
to whistle, spit, stick out their tongues, and some
just quiet, legs crossed in the hot June dusk, not
sweating exactly, just sitting, familiar, and yet
not exactly familiar. And at

the Houston Zoo, June air induces
two giraffes to amatory show. A glance,
like lightning bounced between
the spires of Chartres, shoots through
the gangly calm that otherwise attends them.
The day's all pollen. Sneezing, I almost miss
his great pink party favor
unrolling. Hitting at the height
of their articulate quiet, late-day light

along their yellow length makes little
more than dappled light of their bodies,
light given form, light turned substance
as if by no more than the gathering here
of a cloud of pollen. This is the way,
or almost the way, it feels—yes? or the way we
want it to feel: flesh
gone rarefied into a luminous floating the
bees of us wobble tipsily through
to the flowers of us. No wonder
we're fixed at the chainlink fence with something just
this side of recognition on our faces. And at

the Institute for Biochemical Engineering in Salt Lake,
in its hospital's basement, a test collection
of artificial hearts, opening, closing, on beat
in the water tanks, and the calves next door
with hearts already implanted; and at
the northeast end of Quarryworld, the ocher bricks
being dumped with the hundred high clinks
of glass bottles; and at the rich, black back of
Kathy W.'s garden, the single cucumber
dozing around the hum of its own thin green; and
at the Vent Haven Museum,
the wooden figures of humans, that aren't humans,

saying something for us.

Diagrams

What encourages our belief in the screw as a diagram
of a tornado, is: it's rusty. These sienna clots
in spirals up its threads are exactly the color of Kansas
in miniature, barnsfull of it, funneling up
an early twister's rapid dismantling turns. If it
happened in April, a drillbit frightens you in May,

or a lazy chickenhawk descending its invisible
conch of air. You stop repairing the scattered
barn, for a moment stunned
on the everyday Pretty Prarie red clay, with seeing everything
is a schema of its other-level being. An elm leaf
drying in the sun is a set of directions

toward the staunch-ribbed hull of the Vikings. So
in autumn, dead and burning, it might be a Viking
funeral ship cut loose. The vein that forks
in your wrist is the plan for a dowser's hazel-switch,
it's true, its fulfillment is being pointing in something
that's 96% water. And once, you held a woman's face

in your hands, and though it was dark you read that
chart by touch: how the universe organizes itself
from starfish-arm to the manifold hugs of the outermost
spiral nebula whirling like the wheel-limbed
Indian gods. Her own arms said two mating
chickenhawks organize air like a child's lanyard's being

plaited. It was dark there, on the storm-cellar floor.
It all comes back. You're standing in dust, in May,
staring dumb at a screw on the ground. The winds
were fierce, and she was fierce, and sweet. You think
of DNA. You pinch up the screw from red clay and: it's a
fossil mollusc. Small stone whorl. And simple. Small

stone program of a system.

43

Praise/Complaint

It's a type of time travel—sleeping
then waking a day ahead. I've read enough
disciples of Wells to know how sadly ordinary it is,
a band of night like the shadow a wooden globe's
brass holder casts invariably on one
darkened strip of the world at any moment
—we're all living grammar-school science. Cities
don't blossom like beds of roses in
timelapse movies, the passenger pigeon doesn't
fall like the top shelf of gloves in ladieswear,
there isn't a single 60-year-old executive's wife who
meets a hard young trucker at The Pink Drink who's
her husband 40 years ago—only "now"—stepped
slightly nauseated out of a rift in Time. She'd say
"Just sit here a moment, you look so pale...oh,
waiter!" and later, making fierce
guilty love, a kind of familiarity puzzles her and turns
what she wanted to be a blank violent sexspree,
tender instead. If it happened, she'd look at him
whistle that way while shaving, in part
to tighten the skin for the razor, but also just
from cockamamie happiness, and from the same she'd cry in her hands
and look like a headless woman
going bowling. But of course it
doesn't happen. The new physics nobody
understands, perhaps because it's supposed to be
like Tao and haiku, says that Time can be re-edited,
balled up, taffypulled, but for us it's
this sleep that's never enough, then this waking,
this thing called a day, so hopelessly common and easy.

Then why do we praise it from ziggurat-tops
to tv wake-up shows at 6 a.m. with studio lighting
making little curlicues of rainbow on the coffee the
camera pans into—for this cheap, this almost
consciousless moving-along, why does the shaman

44

axe the hen's behackled neck and welcome
the sun like a sudden inheritance, and my friends
with their one-year-old children in apartments
manylooped-about by freeway systems who
never may see an animal other than alleycat
in their lives but the toy with the string you pull
to make it talk says something called a rooster
goes something like cockadoodledoo and there's
delight in the middle of diapers and mooshing the pears,
what is it, so customary, so simple to slide
right through, yet there's this poundage of complaint,
from every synagogue rises a little stew of breaths that
smell of too much water with too little chicken boiling,
maybe just a breast with a pearl onion nuzzled against it
like a pietà, and it always means a terrible why is being
asked in the face of a terrible silence, what's
this pain that comes from nothing whatsoever,
from only another spate of 24 normal hours, and
the waterbed with its dear-bought lines of coke,
and the duchess's old rococo four-poster, what
pushes us through it and into another so like it
a mother couldn't tell, and the rumpled man who sells
used hearing aids, the model gagging whipped cream up,
the boys with their cars, the wife awake
beside her executive husband shaking 60 years of lovely
graying hair knowing nothing extraordinary will rip
Time open and save her.

In Pain

In pain we populate villages, when it
lessens but lingers, anything
distractive: exactly the color of blue
in a potter's window, a rubbish dump, a pew
the cerulean light breaks into
tenderly, through a saint's symmetrical robe.
It's nearly Christmas; by twilight the lavender,
winter blue in the air, and the Chinese
blue of the potter's glaze, have reached an understanding
like the features of people who sleep together,
face to face, over so many years.
And not much later, they do sleep—Thumb,
the drunk who camps at the rubbish dump, and
the woman the village calls Ducky. In
stillness and chill, they look ceramic. Once,
he scratches his cobalt jaw, that's all. The moon
along her hair could be the moon along the fixed waves
of a porcelain basin, sinuous
but hard. It's another way water can crack
besides ice—an ocean applied in a kiln. And
anyway, there's almost ice; their even breathing
collects in the thinnest blue film. Collects, collects
—no wonder clouds begin to gauze across the moon.
Far off, some carolers...Cool,
a cool blue globe, this whole world, made to press
against your own red hurting. Soon you sleep.
It's summer. Your bed hums with summer.
And on your desk, in the glass paperweight,
a village is being blanketed under
snow like the slow fall of aspirin.

II

A Sanguinary

Mnemonic Devices

The moon, that way of remembering
the light of the sun. The moon, that first gilt
symbol in the margin of the text of the sky.
And then the stars,
those *yahrtzeit*-candles. Everywhere,

the fleshing of fossil
braincells back to slaver, snap, and sing.
The way the taste of blood
remembers ocean, the way the taste
between the legs remembers oceanspawn. My

sister and I become an acronym for: all
of central Europe, its soups, its partidye cloths,
the coins on its eyelids. Music
remembers whole lifetimes. Every
good boy's doing fine tonight. And Roy

G. Biv is getting his formal
whites together, in moonlight
knocks at the door: come on in, I
remember you. This microdot, my
face in row four of a gradeschool photo:

suddenly, under magnification, it
says it remembers all of I'm a
little teapot short and stout, and
what it meant to be shaking onstage at
assemblytime like the waver in teasteam

fogging metal surfaces at the bedside
of a dying man for whom each
pain is an eloquent remembering of what it
was to love a woman in newmown bermuda
beneath the stellar stitchwork when

neither remembered their parents'
admonitions and life was his lust like a
needle playing her lust like a groove and the
record stuck on the sweetest note over
and over—we all remember

that. And then he dies. Each time a
kettle on the stove keens, I
remember him. He joins the hundred fathers
above their hundred fathers above
the lava coal and bonework world of fathers

manifold below me, wholly, each
repeating each, and it's so
lonely here at the tip of the pyramid, talking
to the moon, a priest
responsible for the names of the minions.

---

yahrtzeit: Jewish memorial service

Roy G. Biv: gradeschool mnemonic for the colors of the spectrum, as every good boy...
    functioned in music lessons

Before

The class was History, that's
what I wanted—the bridge
the bent Yid ragman took reluctantly
between steamship and sweatshop, or
older than that: the landbridge
something almost a horse was
grazing its way to Alaska
across on something almost hooves,
or older: something almost a leg
that was the grayveined print of a leg
in a web, before a bridge could be anything
more than a body's own
furthest extension. I was
seventeen. It was sunny. I'd come
from History, and before that
from a lineage of ragpickers,
songpluckers, kettlemenders, renderers
of humpfat for the candles, masters of
disputation over a nuance of scripture,
debtors, diddlers, elegiasts and jewelers
—history too, though the textbook
didn't say it. The page said Presidents
and paper. I wanted something from
before paper—wasps,
the fluted home of their making.
I wanted the first bone
of my bones. I wanted the word
before the alphabet, the word like a suckstone
working up spit. And then I stopped,
near Washtenaw and Ainslie, on the bridge
above the sewerage ditch, and sun
as if meeting a challenge made the stars
of a constellation-story burn
that urban rut's otherwise lustreless
flow. It was the sign of The Cart,
and there too, in the story, sun

bedazzled dull surfaces: all those heaps
of garment-district scraps he peddled,
a few abused tin pots, and who knows
how or why but some wholeskinned Spanish onions,
wool socks, and a single tired rose. I
still remember this: his humming something
tuneless, as if from before the idea of song
took full root in American soil—but
like the rose, though it drooped, though maybe
the worm ate in it, his song was handsome,
a lady would accept it and understand. And
this: my face was reflected, wavery
but ascertainably wide-eyed, on his pots.
Or in the sewerage currents—and then the
stars shifted, light was
sun again, and I was something almost
a man, on its way home,
humming its wanting. I was a boy
with a book. And this was long before
I'd learn to have words for what I wanted,
but what I wanted was something
like a bottle with a notepage in it,
thrown to sea—the clarity of glass,
but from before glass; and the urgency
of that written note, before writing.
—Maybe the water itself,
the message its salt.

Bird

Satificate. That was what my Grandfather's English heard, and how he labeled it. The creases, a century old, are sharp, as sharp as a whiff of ammonia, and they seem to be the replicating image that gives character to the bank where the document's stored: the hard geometry of what money means in America. Teller's smiles you could cut a week-old crust of cheddar with.

Its duplicate information might still be in Germany, in village records stacked in a cellar, beneath its one bulb's drone. A century past, the clerk fastidiously nibbed the information in, the squat black script as heavy as a branch. And a flourish, maybe you could almost say a flower, that was my Grandfather's name. Perhaps the clerk didn't need a new gold tooth after all, or the rashes on the cow's teats went away overnight, who knows? But by that final cursive gaiety, we understand him. Then he went on: somebody's geese for the tax-count, somebody's *zaydee* dead and the coffin cost so much in terms of tins of tallow, somebody's fresh wet field of rye.

And then he'd immediately forget. And then the owner of the geese or the rye immediately forgot. It's what writing's for. It changes the content of an oral tradition's storage system. The brain can afford to give off the aroma of facts in mulch, the glow of facts in foxfire, yes the click of facts in carbon dating.—Somewhere, in documentation, it exists: eternal present tense. Sixteen geese and a rye crop.

I think everyone's known the sensation. You wake—it's dark, and the night and your skin don't show exact delineation. The air is rubbing like a cat at your ear, for admission. Last night I woke— I'd dreamt that I was a limb chopped off a greater body, which still tried to move me and wept. I almost heard the weeping. It was happening in a corner, and there were other sounds, not all unhappy: a fiddle, an animal snort, the thin cool slide of a picture's hanging-wire being positioned carefully on its nail. There was a record kept in the air, in atoms, perhaps in between the atoms, a permanence. I was only a man with his hearing accidentally against that lock's invisible tumblers' turn.

In the spring, a swallow always returns—across the thousand aerial miles, fright and flux, to its own one place. *This* swallow, year after year, to its half-moon hole in the eaves of the court building. See it?—wobbly a moment. This is the year the village is gone. A German village, of tinker Jews, and it's been razed—by fist and by fire. So much char. You wouldn't think the lives of a people had this much ash to start with. Now it's stopped its wobble, it's hovering like a hummingbird mid-air. Above where the records books once were. So calm, so effortless—there isn't a branch but it looks as if it's perched on a branch.

Wings

My parents never took an airplane:
money, caution. I wrote them from France
once: *If you only knew about distance!*
What did I know? They took the Chevy
shopping: milk, a loaf of rye, ground chuck.

There's a photo: I'm between them and we
touch. We face the camera, sun
through leaves makes one lace across us.
—A triptych. Yes,
a central panel and its wings.

The World of Expectations

What starts with F and ends with U-C-K? starts
another stupid high school joke. We also
snapped the thick resilient straps of Maria
Alfonso's bra. I don't know what we expected.
Annoyance, perhaps—though a kind of annoyance
that opened the way for attention—then maybe
intimacy, though we wouldn't have phrased it that way.
We called it F-ing. An alarm goes off,

the expectations are serial and easy: the clumsy
effecting of fire-drill practice, arrival of miles of hose.
And maybe Dennis or Leo or I would get to stand
near Maria, and maybe she'd even bend in her
provocative way that showed the first shadowy
rampway into her cleavage. When I finally did get
effed, of course it had nothing to do with the world
of expectations we mapped round and flat

where the condom ate wallet for years. Now I hear
Leo's divorced; drunk enough, it's as if a large hand
crumples him like a Coors can. The point is, even
Dennis's happiness, what kids mean and a sexual
axis, never struck our daydreams. The point is, not
even sex, necessarily—what did they see
in Station 19 when the bell went crazy? Flames
like cartoon devils? Their heroics, axe and ladder,

tested successfully? Glory? Pain? Some calls to glory
and pain are real, of course. But back then
we pulled levers for hijinks, for stupid jokes. And it came
long, red and clamorous. Firetruck.

The Accountings

1.

So, you want a lot of money. — The way
an old Jewish curse starts, out of the days
of my childhood, when people and sayings were one.
For the guys on the block, it was this: that
if you think of baseball scores while Doing It,
you won't get soft. But all I could think of was
Doing It itself—which meant another world
completely, as I lay in the dark of my parents' house
while they talked love and salaries, Eisenhower
dreamed golf, and far-off unobtainable women
touched themselves when I touched myself, in
mixed-up collages of lipsticked smiles and bras.

2.

No wonder we call them platelets! I want to set
a meal in my heart for everybody I've ever loved.
I want them to sit in those huge red vaulted
chambers, and banquetize themselves happy, and
talk to each other at once—my parents,
the first anthologized poets of my high school years,
and all of the women from 2nd grade's Miss Portney
to my flint-eyed spark-visioned lover-before-last,
under a roof, with enough, at last, forever. Not
that my current lover would understand; although
I think the wish is common: provision; and
the premise is true: the heart's time is simultaneity.

3.

Finally you learn you lose yourself in a moment
larger than you are—all those baseball scores go
floating uncontrollably in magic space. And then
the long "I love you"s with a forefinger lightly winding
sleepiness tighter on each other's skin. We lose
ourselves in each other's skin. There are so many
of us, two seconds of bird in the sky can be a hook that

drags in Ellen Kaufman's quiet anger and ample breasts,
a first selected Whitman, my parents' stern warm
epigram voices . . . and the kitchens of the heart are laboring
mightily to keep up. *May you get a lot of money.*
They meant there were griefs involved—though kept on saving.

Water Pie: Tonight, 12/11/72

Tonight the air's too dry, the vents
offsetting winter cold with the enthusiasm
of retrorockets, until we're dry-mouthed
at the blast and the rims of our nostrils
cake. And in defense we scatter water

filled pie tins through the house;
in sleep, the nose sniffs in a wedge
of water pie, as much as, or more
than, the dog laps at night. Tonight,
when I wake you, my lips burn to lick

your silhouette so that it gleams in moonlight
like halved citrus, want to stop to suck
a flower of blood to your chillest hill
this season, but then continue and touch
you with my expenditure

of this wet as uniformly as it was breathed in.
There's just enough left, a circle
in the aluminum pan, to catch the arid
moon as if it snuck to drink from a gleaming
trap at our bedside. I've no sense,

it seems, of decorum; tonight there are men
on the moon. Well, let them look
down at us if they'd like! We're all
busy, reaching as far as we can,
and perhaps this makes us brothers. I know

when I walk the dog this morning he'll piss
at every tree on the block, his way of claiming
territory with water he's taken in, no pee
in the world smelling just like his. It's
a home. And I sight the sun through his flags,

his warm waves of stink on the cold wind.

And

So you sleep, and I sleep,
close,
very close, but even so
in separate
bands of blackness.
These are the two dark rings

the coon slips off its tail
every night—and just before
morning, returns

with the wild raw taste of strange fish on its mouth

and slips the rings
back on its body again
and we wake

in this life together, make
one animal
showing one mask to the world.

Cross-Country, & Motif Appears

1.
The Volks grows close as a skullcap.
Forty hours—by 11 p.m. near Chittenango
we lose Brook Benton's voice, and static
scratches like a rat to be let from the radio.
We alternate; the wheel marries us
surer than a ring, black sky's our rabbi. Night

vision; retinas, like personal ravens
through portholes, leave our eyes and return
with no twig of destination. Whatever
belief is, it's something to do with the world passing
hazily into morning, sky the color of vichyssoise, and everything
following the centerline like it mattered. Day

means a black pine likened by snow
to a nun, means snow blown moire across blacktop.
Noon means it melts and we're that much closer.
The windshield wiper streaks a slush/dirt arch this
light rainbows fitfully in: a small god, a
small sign of covenant.

2. *"Lord, I believe it's rainin' all over the world."*
                    —as sung by Brook Benton

The road makes everything road. Makes
eyes: a tunnel, road spools into; makes hands
on the wheel: hilled landscape, road cuts. I
look at you (it blurs the world out the window) for
something...a human moue: pout, smile, your own goony
eyes crossed for laughs, or for luck. For luck

we knuckle wood, fling salt, rice, douche in
such-and-soforth solution, kneel
to gods' bodies or who's handy, wish on
candle and bone, beg star. In Anatolia,
at Ararat, they climbed the mountain up
17,000 ice-like-knives feet—for luck,

for relics, pitchy splinters hatcheted from The Ark some
said really rested there glacier-wedged. So
they trudged it, by rope, with pick, and held on
sometimes by no more than thumbnail-width to a cliffwall,
suspended. And so I think of them, for
luck, also clinging to a face.

Vacation: an extended postcard

An hour out of Logan, Utah a stream
is my radio. Half a hot day and into
the chill brush dusk, I watch it doily
foam at its outcrop rocks and smooth
its bedsunk lumps of stone like static
evening meaning out of a songlyric. Call

my parents, and the distance
crackles our talk—the old small
differences between us finally given the honest
excuse of 1,000 miles
of interference. He's retired
and, for my father, his pocketsize police-band

radio is a stream: its rush
of marauding male negroes, moustached six
foot six caucasians who may be armed,
all night, till he sleeps, having monitored
every Chicago alarum, the lull and lap
of urban radio waves. There's a touch of it

even here, just beyond our no
trespassing signs are sounds in the dark
complacent firs—a story of some kid shooting
sudden flash the color of deer but it
called out a name in his father's voice . . . and
what he felt, running up to the first split

second of recognition is something we push
back behind even dream. Most days,
fish are sassy silver shimmies, the cardboard
bear up by the ranger station admonishes us
avuncularly, sky slaps like a nurse
at a newborn's toosh, and last night lifting

fog crowned a bullmoose with seven-point antlers not
40 feet away! And if reception falters, here in the
wild one thinks the antenna buffeted by the wings
of demons attacking, of angels assigned to defend
—how the air of our reaching each other is broken
with trespasses and with patrols against trespasses.

The Form and Function of the Novel

My parents have come to town for my wedding.
Because of some way a shadow falls, or a hand
in conversation cuts air as if laboring, my father
reminds me increasingly of a man in a small
Canadian village, who manufactures racks
for drying lace curtains, who catches shadow in
that same way, and who moves his hands as if against
a current, in a book

I've been reading but leave, to shop
for cheese, bouquets and the wedding trousseau.
While we pick over veils and daffodils, life
according to narrative forces set in motion
continues: the backlands
moon slips up like a washed dish, and a rig
clops heavily toward the main street's tethering-rail.
His son's come home, for that sturdy Canadian

spring with the flowers like nailheads everywhere,
home from study in Europe, his son the biologist
talking Darwin and opera these last two years
over cognac in snifters like goldfish bowls.
They argue. The father is oafish, gruff, a
squared-off man whose lips move reading.
The son knows quiche and genetics. He's
embarrassed. Their words are ugly weather. I

see, although the son ironically can't despite
his interests, how the distance between them is
nothing, you hear me?, nothing, compared to the first
irrepressible land plants over 400 million
years ago stretching familially to the flax
in the lace that's hung in the front display case
under the sign with the father's name but *and*
Son freshly painted out. I think he's special

in his plainness and hurt. In this chapter he's
alone. It's night, he paces in the store he loves, and
so the moon through the fine white nets of his trade
makes him a complicated figure at last,
doilied over by dark and silver, eloquent, pensive, oblique...
"Do you think she'll like this one?" I turn.
He's holding a lace dress up to the late deep light
and it's all I can do to stop crying.

Semiotics/The Doctor's Doll

> *Traditionally, a Chinese physician respected his patient's modesty*
> *by offering her a small doll, sometimes ivory and beautifully*
> *carved, of the female anatomy. She would receive this through*
> *curtains, mark her complaints on appropriate parts, then return the*
> *figure, "examination" completed.*
>
> —Sosho

1.
A small rock braids white water
in blue water. This is why
I think of the stream as a woman
lying face down—that lazy

pigtail, and the little curve
of a waist later on. There even may be
a woman, or man, real, flesh,
nearby for whom this stream is

a summarization—as the desert's red
dementia-spill at sunset, and powder
to cobalt blues of its clearest
daytime heights, became

the shingle in front of O'Keeffe's shack.
There are signs, they say
a thing when a thing is lost
to other saying. This explains

art, and why a peach by O'Keeffe is eloquent
geometry of a kind
beyond a canvas's usual
linear methodology—the inexpressible

ganglia-hurts, star-stitchery and shadow-joys
of a life may find their only shameless
expression in its alive and dying
speckled sexual skin. Or

perhaps it's a mandarin orange
held like a crystal ball, eye-level, that
means the Emperor's favorite concubine's
future—in a garden of tended

waterfalls and peacocks, she's intent
on every ruddy pore, on each sweet meaty wedge
and on the delicate web inside the rind
like a silk map of the nervous system . . .

She's ill. It hurts, here,
and here. For reasons of her own we'll never know,
she considers the orange. For her it's a prophecy
or an insignia or a name. Or after

35 years of sharing the plumbing of heart
and backed-up bathroom, of
the diapersmear and the dollardream and the
intimate spittles of lovemaking, yes my mother's a sign

of my father. When I read her now, her face
the latest turn in a path over
six decades long, I see his face
and its gray lips smiling foolishly

in the hospital room—as if he could keep it
a secret, as if pain were not a red pet
leaping into his eyes, to look out. We'll
visit—kiss him, bring a *Playboy*, kid

about the svelte healthy beauties in there.
And later, alone in my livingroom, I'll stare
without sexuality at the vibrant vaginal lips
of a poster: O'Keeffe's *Grey Line*

with Black, Blue and Yellow in
which two hazy body-shapes define a blue flame
that's a blue petal that's a blue
woman's rich blue sex. So I think of a stream

as a long blue human—yes, with a
scrap of ivory flotsam lodged in a bend, some
doll of what's wrong. Tonight's
symbology says a stream's a person,

so a person's in a bed. My father
weeps and weeps till dawn, in the hospital linens.

2.

Personal names, speculates Jaynes, first appeared between 10,000 B.C. and 8,000 B.C., allowing people to think about a companion long after that person was dead.
                    —Science Digest

Say these nailparings in a matchbox are somebody's
perfect reduction—and under
an incense cone, in sweat, by amber and wavery liquorlight,
a perfect badge of that person's life
is forming out of smoke to fill the room. Do
you believe it? A hundred thousand people believe it.
Say a ring of hair. Say the shaman's soul caught
in a Polaroid, it's ludicrous but
then why is he gasping for air on the mat, for days now?
Everybody's read some version of that story
in which the dollhouse burns, and half a country away
so does the fullsize house it's modeled on. We all
have a doll of ourselves—a child, a wife,
a protegée, taking our tightrope walks and faith healings
into a foreign land. We've all repeated the simplest lesson
of algebra up at the blackboard, teacher
pointing with much-frayed patience at the x, while
we say: *stands-for.* Say it: stands for.
                                        Say
the Master's gospel in proselytizers' ardent
renditions, say the bloodstuffed tampon, say
your own self caught in a Polaroid
25 years ago there like a two-inch doll
at the algebra blackboard, say the sign of a person,
say a name.
            —An old name, Albert, my
grandfather's name and then mine. So now I'm his
ambassador, from a world
of ghetto donkeycarts, fat Sabbath candles, soupsteam
fogging the windows, and a voice in blessing hovering

like God's own special hummingbird over the wine...
—Or older, a clan-name, a cave-name,
Runs-With-The-Bears, Old-Trout-Mouth,
a beast-name, a bird-name...
                              Say she's
Fei Yen, *Flying Swallow*. She undoes
her nighttime pigtail slowly, as if divvying
gold spoils after a battle. And there's been a battle,
in her system, all night. She hears the doctor's pony
stamp where it's tied to the plum in the yard,
she can imagine its breath in the cool dawn light as heavy
as a feedbag at its nuzzle. Her bed is as blue as a stream,
and her azure robe, and the blue brocade that blocks her
from the sight of any male save the Emperor and
his eunuch. Even her slippers are blue, on the blue shelf.
No wonder she looks at the orange. It
jumps like a flame in her tired eyes. And then the hangings
part, and in a pair of polished rosewood tongs
is the doctor's doll. She holds it as a stream
might hold the map of a stream. She runs it
down her body.
                  Once I saw one—an exhibit
at the Denver Art Museum: one entire body done
from one sleek muscle of ivory. She was maybe
a foot long, lustrous and lush, reclining
frankly on a small dark wooden couch—the pale
swell of her nudity framed by a deep blue tortoise comb
in her hair, and sharp black lacquer shoes—civilizing
endpoints. She smiled. Her thighs were coyly crossed.
They made the *x* I must have thought of all the while
my algebra teacher tried to conjure some right answer
out of my adolescence. She told me *x* was a sign
for the great unknown. Man, was it
ever! Then sat back on the edge of her desk
where her lean white hosieried knees were the dials
that tuned in all of my daydreams, she was angry

71

with the things I didn't know, and
so was I, in my own way.
                    Signs,
and more signs, and how to read them. Flashes
like quick carnations of light
in 19th century telescopes—could these be
signs of life on Mars? Could these be the blasts
of canal construction? Signs: the *feng*,
that fantastical bird with the head of a pheasant,
the neck of a swallow, a dragon's wings and a peacock's
ostentatiously plumaged rump: whose appearance
presages virtuous rulers, therefore whose depiction is the
aegis of auspicious reign (one's done in gold and turquoise silk
on her bedcurtains by the Emperor's decree: a *hwang*, a female
feng: "In poetry, many allusions to sexual pairing
are made by reference to the fidelity of *feng* and *hwang*.").
Signs: my grandfather's *yarmulke*, also
silk and also blue—it was the likeness
of the sky his God presided over, and made the most delicate
touch of that glory on his head, for his whole life,
as long as his life was. Now it's mine. And now
I'm his, as the track of a man belongs to that man,
if a track can be left ahead, in ground
a man will never touch, if a track can continue without him.
Often I walk the night and wonder how
many emblems and deputies we make of ourselves, or even
have the empathy to see
in the makings of others. Signs: she was,
as I remember it now, a substitute teacher.
X, she said, on somebody else's behalf. Some nights
I see that mark, in the air, meaning here,
and here.
                    She lets the doll back out
through the curtains. Inkbrushed dots say pain
along its naked length, and say it in hope

72

of pain's negation. Then she sleeps. Sleep feels as if
a giant doctor's hand is holding her, then placing her
in a deep dark pocket. The pony starts its journey...
Say she's my father's name.
Then say my father's name.

3.

In Jewish tradition to this day the name of a person who is critically ill is sometimes changed in order to confuse the Angel of Death.

—Noah Jonathon Jacobs

those clouds in the north
heaving with everything
planet and sky cycle through them
there is a pain in my lungs

this is the leech I have taught
to squeeze itself out
of itself as a symbol
can you help my heart

they give you a number and
then a gown and then a little gauzy mask
I saw him once a cipher
between the check-in and the check-out desk

this is a man on a bed like an entry
written in the book of names
he is Frank he is Red he is Jennifer
he is registered as James

there is no Irving Goldbarth here
there is no Irving Goldbarth here
the needle will wink and the blood will follow
this is the bed of Flying Swallow

this is a prayer I say to the angels
low on insomnia high on dope
dozens of yesterday's specimen vials
are saying a man to the microscope

this is the bed of Flying Swallow
this is the truth now disappear
this is the bed of Flying Swallow
there is no Irving Goldbarth here

The British in Africa

"... formula, ritual saved them"

Black coffee beats at the heart of a day
at your life's most desperate: and two lumps say
all you need to know about how much
sweetness will carry you through to nightfall.
And enter, and face what you must, and shaking
hands with the undertaker, you think of tea served

daily at 4 in the china cup on a magistrate's mid-jungle
verandah, something out of a Joyce Cary novel you read
ten years ago; and you realize every hand shook
sitting *shiva* acts as a momentary rung
up a terrible rockface. And when you wake
alone in bed for the first time, the first thing

you do's brew a pot. Now, somewhere, darkness
shadows an unmapped veldt ravine, and cold wind cuts
through muscle as through a strawman's chest,
a chasm where some man could lay his blueing cheek
on the bottom brush and gibber and sleep lost
even to air-search in such unruly tangle. But you

grip safe to doorknobs, faucets, and dress
like the British in your own version of formal whites;
a new day's undershorts, catching you, this
net above where the drop is deepest.

A Sanguinary

1. Michael's

With his white cap and its perfect chain
of ancient sweatmountains rounding it.
With his cleaver in the air, with his cleaver
in the meat—the cleaver doesn't care.
Whomp Whomp. He halves the
marbled buttend
of a corned beef into an animal
geode.

This is someone's father.

This is the sudden-come understanding that
passes enlightenment to a 13-year-old: everyone
has a father. This is my
friend Michael's.
Nyah-nyah *nyah*-nyah *nyaaah*-nyah
Mi-chael's *fa*-ther's *bloo*-dy

With his whole red side of a steer
on his back, with his whole bent bunched
piano-mover's back. And in fact
the ribs are set in the raw meat like raw keys.
Up the plank to the cooler.
With his pacing at night in that lavish
cathedral of freon; with the hooks like questionmarks
God's asking back; with the ice
gargoyles and belfries. Pacing,
monologue grumble CASH ONLY.
Someone's father holding a bowel-like-a-fire-hose.
Playing canasta. Five o'clock shadow like tacks
driven up from inside. At night, a pat
along a son's head with a hand too blunted to feel.
This is the smell of blood under his nails, even.
This is someone's father
with his work, with his apron of blood on.

2. Pressed Flowers

There came a time when understanding was taught
to be facts. Pierre,
South Dakota. The shadow of Earth
on the moon. The Earth and the moon
were pool balls. Janice Netter's breasts
were an ache in my own chest. Janice
Netter's breasts were the size of pool balls,
hard and white. I would have died
for their shadows. There were charts
and pie graphs. The Circulatory System
was a great tree in a man. Those red
cough lozenges were blood cells. So
the days went by, in models
of knowledge. Sodastraw
molecules. Plaster of Paris
Paris. So the nights went by, dreaming
Janice Netter. I wanted a kind of spice,
I suppose, like a kind of Columbus. And she
was a kind of new world. There were tests,
1) what a giraffe eats, 2) what a tribal unit is,
3) define a satellite. So the years went by.
At night a boy on the verge
could lift his hand in front of his eyes and wonder
subatomic pipecleaner structures whirling
away like crazy in there. I wonder
it still. There were tests,
in shame, in crumbling under first anger, in seeing when
strength meant turning away.
There were blushes, and uncontrollable
uplunges of the cock. This was the blood-tree
from Biology, only real, and this
was smackdab fullforce Spring. It bloomed
enormous, lush rashes of flowers.

*

So we were 13.
    The cells of the body,
all of the cells of the body, are new each
seven years, and what
pressed flowers in part
survive such slough and flux, we call
our memory.
     Michael calls;
his father's died. His father, Papa Joe
from when I was 13.
       I've sloughed
three selves since then. Though I'm older
than he is by 21 years, that wimp kid
in the bar mitzvah album, smiling with my face
inside his face like a diver two or three inches just
short of surfacing . . . See? In a way,
he's my father.
     Papa Joe
above a sirloin shaped like Asia, Papa Joe
who gave me the fat loud spattered necktie
in my closet and it's back in style,
Papa Joebelly, Mr. Papa Joe. Michael's voice
with thin cracks in it. He tells me
his father's heart attacked.
       That photo album
self of me . . . it's gray, between the pages
like a flower in an encyclopedia volume
for 21 years. And I have an assignment tonight,
a homework. I'm to look up
everything I remember of one day
         when
I looked up from a diagram
in my biology text, and there was
Papa Joe's work-apron hung on the wall
with its stain in the same shape.

*

When you concentrated fully on the blood-tree,
when you stared with red intensity at the blood-tree,
you saw everything else
was only a kind of weather around it
—the flesh and the muscles, all the pearltipped
pins of pain, the fatty swags of passion,
that gray cloud floating the bough—
weather around the blood-tree, just
a touch of breeze in its branches.

3. *What a Giraffe Eats*

High leaves.
How It's 15-18 feet tall.
How Simple. It stretched out

  over generations. Now it has a system
  fit to its needs. Now it's a landscape
  for the redwood
  of the blood-trees. In their field work

"Investigators learned much
from the electrocardiograms of whales and from
heart failure in cattle at thin-air heights"

  because the gray pea prostate
  just the *nth* part of the body
  can fill
  with hurt enough for the whole of the body

  because the beauty
  up the retinal thread from an eye
  will fill the brain
  will fill the three pounds of the brain

How There are levels and accommodations
  There are understandings and confusions

  too large for a single human life
  and so they fit
  in the greater human life, they stretch out
  over generations

One time, in the Houston Zoo, I saw two of them
mating—like neighboring castles
and one rolled out a red carpet of welcome

into the other. Everybody
gawked. It was a comedy and glory
everybody knew, on a level they'd
never know. And a woman next to me said *It's*
like bursting in on your parents
doing it—earlier creatures,
speaking your tongue.

"Analysis of giraffe blood has shown
that its chemistry is not grossly different from that
of human blood."

*

And we learned that William Harvey traced that system,
down its many hammers and one amazing fist.
                                                    It's
—oh, say 1625. /I *profess*
to learn and teach anatomy/ He's back from a turn
in the wards at St. Bartholomew's /*not from books*
but from dissection/ and he's tethered the roan
outside his lime-mucked pigeon coops /*not*
from philosophers but
from the fabric of nature/ and now in the dusk
of a day of rheum-oozing Grub Street ginswills,
someone's grandmama with a breast
sawed off, that small girl gored by a boar,
and her master squeezing the yellow French Pox pus out
from the buboes on his stump...
                                        now Harvey
enters the cool clean shadows of his Menagerie
under the dovecote, and is lost observing the chick
still in its shell, the definite
network in the transparent
paisley a shrimp is, all of the pumps the size
of pollengrains, in bees,

slugs, worms, the castanet clackings of oysters, and here's
a pig tied on its back to a plank
and its living belly cut
open as neat as window shutters,
                              and
here's the Physician Extraordinary to James I,
William Harvey, having published his complacency-shaking
study of the looping of the blood, in 1629
defending it—over a blue-hued charsweep's body
bladed gaping and clamped back, Harvey
with his wax-tipped stylus traces
up the curlicue
gray doodles in the wrist, the sturdier tubule-runs
through the arm, to the chest, where they write their recycling
s- and y-shapes in this candle-lit lick
of the human lung, in this guttering dissection-room's
disclosures of the aeon-perfected sanctum-rooms
at the heart of the human heart.
                              And
what would even that expert student of anatomy
say at the miles inside a giraffe? In Africa, what
would even William Harvey say in the *outré* face
of bushbuck, springhare, hippopotamus,
steenbok, dik-dik, kori bustard, eland, gembok,
hartebeest, wildebeest, kudu, the ostrich made
seamless from incompatible parts...
                              We'll never
know. I like to think him wearing away wax-headed
stylus after stylus in inching his studious way
along the giraffe's vast cardiovascular map, and
saying, not much surprised, "It
is not grossly different..." and maybe
stroking the neck, the flanks, as he would
his roan's, with a brusque affection.
                              What
the Bantu say in the African bush, without the diagrammatic

aid of the Darwin-tree, its forkings
a finesse of interspecies consanguinity, monkey
here, and *here* giraffe, and way down *here*
the worm, and up *here* man at the apex ... I'll
never know. But there are hunting songs
that call these other beings
"brother," "sister," ask permission, joke,
solicit advice.
                In the Bantu
rite called "being-born-again,"
the father butchers
                        a ram
"and three days later wraps the boy
in the animal's stomach membrane
and skin." He'll be a fullgrown
male of the tribe, and marry, and kill, and wear the masks,
and carve the ironwood sticks, but
first he must be swaddled three entire days
in the sweet ram stink, must be its heart and its heart's
voluminous transport, must be
birthed
as if in actuality cut away
from a kind of ur-ancestral he-beast
umbilicus and bloodworks.

*

Or what the Nativity means: at one time
there were animals
closer to God (they could lick Him)
than you'll ever be.

*

"At birth—I've never told
anyone this before ..." then Michael stops.

Yes? "...Well, I had a screwed-up
RH factor. And what they had to do,
my pediatrician pioneered the technique, was fill me
by transfusion, completely, every
last scraggle of day-old capillary,
with my father's blood."

There's a pause. Something leaves him
then enters him again.

"They strapped us down and drained me out and
then they poured him into me. You're

a poet—just think about
that blood

       stretched out
       over generations

4. *What a Tribal Unit Is*

We don't know.
But we think they looked like this, and this,
when hunting. We have chalk flints.
We have wild cattle done
in red ocher on limestone walls with
angular incisions that may be spearheads.
We have a pit the bison were
stampeded into, and evidence of
organized lugging away of cuts of bison,
and so we think we know

of nights around a fire, planning
something in common and in a common tongue.
We don't know. But we have the remains
of the fires. We have an idea of what a night is
with the bear outside, the ravenous bear of the caves,
and what a fire means
in night like that, and the vertical stories rising
up a fire, we think they hunkered a circle around the fire,
holding hands. We have the hands

on the walls, done hand on hand, by blowing the paint
through tubes. We have the shit and we can read it,
it's a single diet
floating in many stones. And
there were rites. Before the first rough lumpish pots
or coins or nets or little burial boxes

we think there was song, we think by a grotto lamp
a boy was notched, in onehood with his people.
We don't know. But in the scatter of unworked stones
they used for lamps with a wick of juniper twig,
is one lamp worked in a smooth
and moving sweep, out of deep-rouge sandstone,
this would seem to say

a ceremony. We think that stories of spirits
were handed down, of spirits and stars. We think
the "handing down" of literal importance, the idea
of hands in red paint on a wall and what
it means for understanding
something passes like a torch or a shell of water
down a line of men in

time as well as in space—that there are
generations, and stages in a generation, and moments
to mark a stage. We don't know. But
we have the ox-ribs carved finely in regular groupings
of 30—the moon? a menstrual record? and
we can see in microscopic study
these were held, and held again, and worn
in handling, then their images
refreshed, as if a moment came in torchlight
when the song rose up to take a form
that kept the dark at arm's-length, and the words
they said were "This is for you now,
This is what we know and now you know it, Take it,
This is what a tribe is, You will also pass it on,
In time that's your time."
We don't know. But we do

have their hands in museums,
like fingerbone Japanese fans.
Like opened, white, bone fans, on wine velvet. Not a one
is essentially different from my hand.

*

So they showed us movies.
Australia, Africa.
Bantu boogajoos dancing up a storm.
I remember, one was called
"The Dark Continent." It was 1961. We were

13. I studied
Janice Netter sitting in the movie darkness, everything
of mystery and foreigness
I wanted to explore.

*

And Janice Netter traced that system.
And Sharon Feldman traced that system.
And Ava Brecker with her girlish books on horsewomanship
and the little chocolate nougats that caught on her braces
traced that system, as sure as William Harvey,
surer. They laughed. They had notes
and were excused. They had little brochures from their mothers
with flowers on the cover, in pastels.
We all had Fabian's big hit "Lonely Teenager."
Davey had a playing card with a naked lady and got caught
in Geography showing Richard Jaskoulka
her big tits one at a time. We said big tits a lot.
We taunted Ava Brecker. It must have been horrible
that first time, all the pain in some layer
that never registered pain before, and then the half-understood
flow. They had a network of lore
and emotional support, I'm sure, that functioned
in the ladiesjohn beyond those brochures with the lilacs.
Hey, Big Tits, Big Tits. We hurt each other.
Mi-chael's *fa*-ther's *bloo*-dy. I got a fat tie. From Papa
Joe, he gave me a fat red tie, and ties were thin then.
Sputnik was big then. We got lectures on some scientific spark
touched off by Sputnik once a week. I began my
bar mitzvah lessons. I memorized the Hebrew.
"Col Amar" it began, or something like that. They
wanted me to sing it with a passion I devoted to
my late-night-walk renditions: "I'm a
LONE-ly TEEnay GERRR." I didn't want to.
I fought. In those days late-night-walk meant 8 o'clock.
And then in bed by 10. Janice Netter a ghost girl

in my arms. *"Jew-Weenie-They-Cut-It-It's-Teeny."* Mine
was learning to be enough. By day it hummed. By night I
experimented. For Science Fair, Michael and I
constructed a wheel a mouse turned with an electrical gadget
we rigged up to look like a Sputnik. I don't think I ever
realized the strangeness, thinking astronauts then
going home to practice the millenia-old bar mitzvah.
Rabbi Lehrfield spit when he talked. "But do it
for Grandma Nettie," they said. "You know she hasn't long."
Geometry was looong. I cried in class once. Ava Brecker
wept then whinnied in fear like one of those horses she read about.
I read. They laughed, I read so much. I had glasses
by then and Neil Somebody always pushed them
into the bridge of my nose, *hard*. So I understood why
I needed to follow Ava in a pack of boys and go
Big Tits, Big Tits. Her pants were white that day and the
stain so red it's close to jet in my memory. Maybe we
all understood. It lasted, like Geometry,
forever. We couldn't even put that mystery
into language—Tits, we said. Big Tits. Biology
told us this and that, but in those days sex education
meant flowers. There was a hefty chapter on The Circulatory System
and a chapter on The Secret Life of a Tree
and they looked the same. I looked like—here,
like this, that's my father on the left and his mother
my Grandma Nettie a year before she died. Co-OLLL
A-MAAAR. I think I could sing it
today and mean everything poignant that's happened since then,
three sloughs of the body ago. I have my high school yearbook yet,
and my biology text. They also look the same
by now—an overview
of beings and their blood. I could go to my closet right now,
where it's still on the hook as if my own father
had given it to me.
That huge red tie.

*

Silhouetted black
against a clear cream sky,
to our eye
the giraffe is the shape of someplace holy,
massive, Chartres . . .
                    If birth
requires blood, the "being-born-again" requires
blood again:
                    a ram
is strung up by the hindlegs, and its stomach
is being prepared: a three-day wombsac
for the "fetus-again." The smell is a
waxy solid.
                    Follow that
churchly giraffe, and it won't be long we'll come across
a tribe for which oblation-blood is
human:
            I have a photo of
"an aboriginal novice," a boy,
he's kneeling under an elder of the tribe, whose veins are opened
"to incorporate him
into the society of men,"
and it's flowing in ribbons,
in actual rivulets, viscous and rich, down the boy who
looks like a teakwood candle-holder
a candle of blood has melted
wholly over.
            I have a photo of
my cousin Alice's firstborn
in a loafsized wicker basket, with the rabbi bent to the small swipe
of dexterity a circumcision knife requires, meanwhile the initiate
is sucking wine from a twisted napkin teat—and around the table,
my face included, by implication
my own notched cock included, festive,
fearful, joking, holy, and in empathetic wince—see?
the society of elders is gathered to witness.

*

This is what I see: the shape of the sacred.
Maybe a giraffe is kneeling,
making a single, urgent, stylized
spire, as if anybody, of any persuasion, were welcome
here to worship.
                              It's midday. Parrot,
rhino, cheetah. The river is old,
so old it's red, the deep dramatic red of borscht
in an East European *shtetl*...A boat in the distance.
A man in the boat...Or, no—an even older
red than that. The most
ancient of rivers.
                              William Harvey's
boat grows larger. He's tracing this system.
Every tributary, every fine red thread, he has
a calipers and an astrolabe and a diviningrod
and he wants every backwater whorl of this river
mapped to its source and recycling.
                              Now he
puts into shore where the line of trees
is most enormous. These are the ancient of trees,
he knows it, these are the great, original, pumping
heartwoods and their branches. The roots are
jeweled with grubs. The boughs are a jabber of primates.
These are the trees that drink
directly of the river, and William Harvey wants to explore.
He walks in. There's a quiet. In the quiet
there's a man, in a rag of shade, he's stringing
an animal up by the haunches.
There's a bowl below the throat, and there's a blade
in an official obsidian handle, and this is
somebody's job. This is a man
who's going to make a line, dividing
life from meat. Harvey wonders: madman?
priest? everyday neighborhood butcher mumbling?
Or maybe that's a prayer. Or a cry that's
older than prayer. With his swing through the air.

With his face besmattered.
Washing the knife off now.
—Somebody's father.

5. *Define a Satellite*

On some nights I go for a walk and the moon
isn't there. It must be in the past
for a moment, as if turning back to an old text
of itself, the stages, trying to get down straight for one more time
how it's done. And when I go through that blankness
block by block, I think of the people who aren't here for me
that same way,
                 knowing they'll be
faces come into a fullness
lighting everything,
eventually, in their time, by a calendar
the nuclei of cells may keep but
numbers will never account for.
If I wander then, in reverie as much as in a maze
of golden raintree and mimosa, thinking Papa Joe this
and Papa Joe that, I see
                 first,
in a seeing as jagged as it is, that Paleolithic/Neolithic
knife, from the catalogue to a show
of Judaean antiquities—just two intentional edges
away from being another dumb stone. It's this
five inches of flint that must have
koshered the throat
with a few quick flicks to supper's
jugulars, mumble-and-bless,
                 this one
not different from one when "Joshua
made him knives of flint
and circumcised the children of the Tribes
at Gibeath-ha-araloth, Hill of the Foreskins."
It implies a cube of fossil hands
about it, from the first
appointed butcher's efficient hack-and-trim
to the curator's fusses, as literal as the hunk

of flint that also, at one time,
held it.
      I see him,
lighting the first friezed terracotta lamps in a
ceremonial line, then working the blade
from out of the oxskin sheath it
worked from out of the ox...
             And then I think what
does Michael think.
           I believe it's the moon.
Yes, Michael with his own birthweight
of fatherblood in him, Michael with 6 pounds 7 ounces
of fatherblood in him, in orbit.
           I believe
it's the moon. And when it reaches fullness
in the brain, no matter how long the cyclical absence, then
its light transfigures everything, and Michael
must walk out too, beneath the trees, and see whatever
world that's showing through the darkness
speaks of fathers, calls the father
in his system into a steep
outreaching crest,
          as I've seen Janice Netters
time and again break over the sheet
with the woman in them that's been called into its own
periodic crescendo.
          I believe it's the moon
swollen full as a tick in the branches
of live-oak, redbud, silver birch and banana
tonight, the moon in the lake like a leech
in a jar, medicinal, plump, disgusting, the moon
and the blood and a certain ripeness making
for commerce between them.
          I believe tonight
he's walking as I am, donors
out into the piercing light, the moon

in the elm, the moon in the olive,
crepe myrtle, catalpa, cherry and yew,
those resinous sexual creatures, acacia, pampas-huggers, asphodel.
I believe the moon will make itself known in the bough
of a man as easily as in poplar,
larch, pecan and weeping willow, the manifold
banyan and the unashamed dwarf pine, I believe
a man is a tree to the moon, I believe
in moments of great transfusion.
                                    There
are old barns in Vermont, from paint poured straight
from the animals' rent necks, and in winter
the only thing not white is a conversation
between barn-red and ever-green around it,
I believe this is the language of the moon we sometimes
overhear and a word or two makes
tantalizing sense,
                    I believe
the bloodhound howls a syllable of it, the cypress
understands the scent on the rag, and the fig,
and the fir, and the hilltop maple.
I believe I can feel it in me tonight,
tree of my current body,
blood-tree
rooted in me and seeming to cast
three shadows:
the bodies I've sloughed up to now.
They're walking with me,
clear in this light, three bodies
that look like but don't look like me.
And behind them, faintly, yes
now, taking shape, here...
all of the other bodies.

Ssh

I know: your pain, its having rooted
in. Well even now, on a small
Sicilian farm, they're shooing the chickens
together into a fecal-smudged, ruffled clump.
They're not much but I give them to you,
prescriptive. I give you a brush dipped
thick in its black ink, like a child
falling asleep one summer afternoon,
his head dipped into the black
China skies. I give a dream
brushed heavy in black ink: coal,
obsidian, crows on a wire,
notes of jazz on the line. It's
night in China. I know: your pain.
It's bright out: the chickens are
shaking off great chunks of light,
like retrievers out of a pond, but
even so: they're finally secreted
in wicker baskets and blanketed over
with odd scraps from the sewing bin.
Even the wind, that rummaging
hand in the green till, is hushed in its
olive boughs. I give you the darkness the
pit knows, in the meat, in the oils,
the dark that's the home of the seed.
I give you the rabbi's cap, the nun's
jet wimple, the pocks on the dice,
no matter the sun: I give you the black
of a panther, of the retina
the panther courses and
disappears into, the retina
behind its lid, the black of the awning
closed and the city in silence. Now
they've lowered those baskets,
by noon, down the dry well. Those
chickens will never call the sharp

attention of the king's men
to this town. It's okay now. They're
passing right by, with their lances.
They're passing right by this
stone throat of sleep at mid-day.
I give you that sleep. I blanket you over.
No matter the sun. I know: such pain.
It's passing right by. Your feather pillow.

III

Chronologues

Witch Trial, Transcript

"White spikes: the bones
of blades of grass
twiddled in the air above The Village
at my command, a supernatural weather,
sometimes they fell on the puffy burgher
bodies like jaguar teeth, tiny arrows
that point to a place too far to be named,
though some took the journey, do you remember
what Goodman Tobias finally coughed
up, what kind of wet webmarks it left?;
but sometimes those barbs just jangled
amid the steeples when I gave word, and rubbed
together like any man and wife
honing themselves, sharpening their silverware
fingers, using each other as blades
to breathe on, to check whether they are alive,
I have seen them polishing each other's talons
by the blue light that shines in the refuse dumps.
What harm could I do with such tiny magic knives,
eh? plug the hornpipe's holes? scratch evil
runes on the psalter covers? or sever more
than the gray vein in an infant's neck?
And most of the time they rode harmlessly
pierced through the flying excrementa"
                                she said
on the thirteenth day of the trial. The judge
said: "The mole below her left teat is a suckhole
whereby her witches familiar, called Mushroom, drank blood
for its nourishment. This she admitted
aloud in the dungeon before a sworn body of witnesses
when the prosecutor applied the aforesaid rat
Mushroom to her breasts."
                        On the first day
she said: "I have never caught the Devil's cold
prick in my lap, my dress could never lift so high
that Satan would clamber under disguised as an innocent

shepherd boy at a circus. Even the animal-organs I rub
in flesh-cuts of the hill folk heal
with no more smoke and writhe to them
than the philtres of the King's own physician.
Those parts were lies. I never clawed up
the greased pole in the poplar glade and pissed
in a corpse mouth, or wore a goat's head,
or danced, or sang."
                                        The children said:
"She landed in the circle and everybody was
you know, not wearing bedclothes.
Then she bent over like she was going to what
we cannot say, but you know, and everything
there be it human or bestial kissed her you know
where, and so we ran away. She was keening things
you can imagine." The judge
said: "The sight of the Holy Bible has worked blessed
miracle on the prisoner who, merely by viewing
a blush-tinted sketch of The Virgin, confessed
to the kidnap and the burnt-offerings on the third day
of her attachment to the Rack."
                                        The children said:
"When she hung down from the alder-bough her hair,
each hair, wrote something in the dirt we dare
not repeat lest lightning strike our tongues
but we thought we read the name of Mayor
Allkirk good man may his soul rest forever
undisturbed by a curse, we thought it was his name
or a trick of moonlight perhaps, the moon
was full. We were too scared to see
what the cat gnawed." The judge said:
"On this twelfth day of the trial the prisoner
voluntarily does penance for her crimes
against the Church and for the cow-sacrifice
and for her ministrations at the bucket
altar discovered in her backyard, not
only by continuing the week of forced starvation
by her own will, but by falling,
every time we stand her up, to her knees

with head bowed." On the thirteenth day
the witch said: "It's your own stake
gives me the strength now to stand
before you with a straight back.
It's your own fire gives me the sparkle eyes
need to cast a hex. It's a witch
of your own making, curses you: may
you know what, and your offspring too,
and around the wrists and the genitals."

Duly recorded testimony. Everyone said the hens
lay larger eggs now, Goodman Fletcher also
has stopped strapping his wife's back
with the horse reins, the winter also is short
now, and only the milk of every fourth cow
or fifth has them green spots, and almost no women
need be scarred with hot irons for green spots
now that the witch been gone.
                              The children said:
"What good was it to be a berry
hanging on the outermost fringe of everything
familiar to us, without a typhoon
to flap like a hawk trapped in brambles,
a plunge to the crooked road
leading to The City, or one scarlet period
staining a crossroads while the hare ran
west over flatland with a berry seed
travelling east through its guts?
Really that is our secret language. Really
we were only standing hands linked
in the woodpatch with the day's chores,
stumps split and hatchets stropped, forgot
at our backs; it was dusk; we were only
looking up into one more night, waiting how
long for a Great Meteorite to plash in the deep liquid
center of our lives
                    and so we said
she was flying."

DIALOGUES:
Johann Joachim Winckelmann and Joseph Busch

Which wonders? First, living Dresden and I,
official ambassador and scholar's spy from that city,
set down in Pompeii unperturbed
at the night sky lit; I seemed at home
amid statuary so exquisite bronze
tears almost flowed and lead cheeks flushed,
I seemed back home beneath the Dresden heavens
in flame with Circus fireworks. Second,
that this delusion lasted but seconds, here
it was 1767, I was in Pompeii, the art
treasures' bronze eyes stared through air
at the sky for their first unearthed time
in 1700 years, and the sky for them seared the same
now: Vesuvius; gone from Dresden a dozen years
digging roofs away for the rare look
down into skulls of Pompeii artisans, I could see
finally what their last sight was: fire

Apprenticed at ten, so an art restorer 73 years, and my father
before me. So it was. The van, en route to Schieritz for safe-
storage of paintings, stopped overnight in Dresden on the Elbe
Embankment. It was 13th February 1945. I remember the
driver: Schmidt. How I tried to explain the use of the aqua-
marines to him, and he only wanting a night's rest from my
talking. I went on through Schieritz alone to make arrange-
ments, but the lights and the burn, you could feel them stare
through your back like rivets. When I returned on 14th February,
they were gone: 158 oils, including the delicate Courbets. And
Schmidt, and the van, and everything else gone to ash and
slag in the heat of the heart of the fire-storm.

east to west, streetstones to stars, nothing but blaze
from wick-hot trees along the horizon to hair
aflame on their arms. This time, this 27th time
the world burst through Vesuvius, we lived;

unlike the year 79, woke sleepers did not count
the herd of 600 sheep dropped bleating down
a fissure, the silver fish skeletons did not fly
like torched ghost-galleons over the Baths, no
birds fell diving like fish into 50 feet
of lava, or people—slaves and senators—thrust
arm-bone through ribcage, linked thus in death
indistinguishable, twisted ash-gray or fume-green
monogram of lost names. And yet, even now,
in this lesser blast, it was easy to see why
one entombed Pompeiian waiting for windpipe
to plug with pumice, would scratch out
'Sodoma Gomora' with claw to clay wall,
certain this could only be God's retribution
to Emperor Titus for crazed maltreating
Jew-citizens. Even now, the volcanic pine-tree
shaped cloud Pliny reported rose up the blood
red sky above us: while we above life

They say first what the Allies called 'Christmas-tree' flares
marked out the bombers' target area. The flames dead and the
melted faces pried off concrete, we could see what it was,
though we only guessed then: 'the largest single massacre in
European history.' I think, apt punishment for the Jewish mil-
lions, in only the mind of an accountant-God. He didn't see
the entombed done up stiff and metal-blue as piping. If He
did, He didn't lift them up. They were serous. Stinking liquid
leaked out. It rose up the steps twelve inches.

of the ancients, life of our ancestry,
life preserved perpetually in stasis
and petrification, we shivered
quicker than earthquake accounts for. Other
wonders? we continued digging: gold
attracted the Italian court to uncover,
sift, and claim. For me, the coins found
scattered where first dropped, were symbolic
of commerce between my Dresden's shops
and the marble counters of this world—still

intact, underground, still in context, it seemed
still warm with the touch of routine—and its familiar
business and pleasure. Those coins: we guessed
by explicit pictures of specialization
colored in above each cubicle, what was the service
for which gold passed to baubled Smyrna,
Aegle, Maria, the *asinellae*, 'little donkeys,'
whose names were scratched over the bar.
I have read *Fanny Hill*—her mother's mother's . . .
We guessed what rumble in the earth it took
to distract from a man's own low rumble:
the gold coins still unearned, the girls more stripped
and open to the night now than a man could dream . . .
And, true, we would swear the world was sleeping

A few of the surviving R.A.D. girls told of the Carnival per-
formance at the hospital for legless soldiers. The Maidenführerin
of the unit, she told me 'I never realized corpses would shrivel
so small in intense heat.' They would find their own boyfriends,
charred, three feet long. In one hostel they dug out ninety
girls of another R.A.D. unit. She said 'They just sat there, as if
stopped in conversation. Even cutting their underclothes for
samples for identification, it was hard to believe they were
not alive.'

and soon to wake, wrap toga, warm tripod, enter
avenue, and greet us as strangers, the life
was arrested that fresh and fleshy!: 'Everyone
writes on the walls—except me.'—This
smeared on a wall near the *odeon*, the concert theater,
where one relaxing Roman corpse clutched jug
as if to invite our tongues and toasts. Of course
I was eager for Piaggio's contrivance of pig-bladders,
winches, and silk thread, rigged for unrolling
charred manuscript-scrap; we had the statues,
the marble satyr coupling-to-come with goat,
the dew-hued limbs of the youth Reginus I restored
with new-chiselled flowers in his hand replacing the original
reins he held for a marble horse now missing; these

we had, and now, with the documents' debut,
the song, the murex-scent, the theorem,
that thereby would be also revealed! It was easy
often to forget this was no longer thriving
city, but museum, no longer tribunal, but tomb

Maybe the Dresden Opera was worst, that contrast, those
people dressed in their finery; their wedding rings gleamed in
the tumbled dark. We dug: gas masks were needed, sometimes
cotton soaked in alcohol to avoid the stench; by May 6, we
had 20,000 rings, cut off bone with bolt-croppers. Next to
people: the Circus animals; forty-eight horses littered one
street. Escaped from the zoo, a flock of vultures descended.
The beaks snipped like shears.

> where the step of our own lives echoed
> amid a mere semblance of life: on the wall of the Villa
> dei Misteri, the mural mistress hugging phallus
> seemed no longer painted decoration, but sad planned
> contrast with our plaster cast of that household's mistress,
> pale and other-worldly, posed curled on the floor.
> Against her breast, the smaller skeleton of a girl
> —her daughter?—pressed futilely for refuge,
> also curled, as if in preparation to enter
> by persistence a mother's belly and breathe forever
> the foetal dark. So easy to understand
> how knowledge that flight meant safety was nevertheless
> repressed by the urban urge to cling like this girl
> to a hand, a human chest, or only a wooden chest
> perhaps, a bag of jewels or a floor plan, to remain
> trapped under roof through this strange fatal freedom
> of choice. Not only the people: the pets,
> a globule of dog, once chained, then choked, now splintered
> bones implying the muscles' curve of convulsion
> about a tethering-post. The shackled bones
> of slaves were not much less in death than our own

One shape I will never forget was the remains of what had
apparently been a mother and child: shrivelled and charred

into one piece, and stuck rigidly to the asphalt. Prised up, you
could see the child's small outline, beneath the mother, the
mother's arms clasped around it. Neither could be identified.
So many were afraid to run outside through the fires; it would have
saved them. They died this way interred in tunnels, cellars, underground
shelters. Their homes were their graves. Saddest were prisoners in
cells who died, or the British prisoners on recovery detail forced to
enter the scenes of greatest putrefection. The two major risks weighed
heaviest on them, but we all shared the fear of these: epidemic, or being shot for looters 'even if nothing suspicious is found on their per-
sons.' But who would want those rings?

> work gangs of convicted Barbary pirates
> in leg-irons, iron spades gripped for salvage.
> And this wonder saddened me most. It was greed,
> these scavengers in ransack for somebody
> else's goblet, ring, barette, broach, or slave
> wages earned in similar worker's labor,
> that prompted the regent Tonucci to order
> the whip and galley for thieving; to save
> these treasures for the court's own
> thieving greed; at first it was all I could to steal
> sketches of lesser Pompeii mastery, free
> for home view and Saxon allegiances;
> it was a war, I was the Dresden army, how
> men thus embroil themselves I cannot
> comprehend, partake though I must. But
> now, one last night at the inn, my new
> found friend will guide me shortly home
> to Germany with my gain, and I can lean
> with leisure again against the modern world
> and think such questions through: histories,
> do they interconnect? in the true *milieux*
> are there ways of viewing destruction

Finally, in March, a zoo lion found feeding in the shadows;
bodies bulldozed into mass graves; or burned at the pyres in
Altmarkt Square. There, they say, in 1349 the Margrave ordered
burned at the stake, the city's population of Jews. You cannot

stop a cycle; it only reverses, and finally reaches you anyway. Shrove Tuesday Carnival day: the day the Jews burnt six centuries ago, and also the day their avenging bombers attacked: 13th February 1945. When I returned on the 14th, it was Ash Wednesday. The dead were rising on pitchforks and picks.

and reconstruction akin? There must

Note: Winckelmann (1717-1768) German-born self-made scholar, called "The Father of Archaeology." He was sent from Dresden to study the closely guarded excavations at Pompeii and Herculaneum (destroyed and buried by volcano, 79 AD). The theories and practical suggestions in his ensuing reports, although many proved to be incorrect, influenced the philosophy of generations of art historians and the field techniques of all archaeologists thereafter. In 1768, returning to Germany via Trieste, he was murdered in an inn over a number of gold and silver medallions awarded for his services. He never lived to publish an account of his 1767 witnessing of Vesuvius' latest eruption; his last written words: "There must." Much of the factual material here reported by Winckelmann was actually unearthed long after his death; and his reveries are my own imposition. Joseph Busch (1858-1948), an elderly German art restorer, is a character of my fancy; but these selections from his "memoirs" are arranged from quotes from witnesses and/or official reports as given in David Irving's *The Destruction of Dresden.* Allied aircraft destroyed not only that German cultural center; in 1943, mistakenly believing a German panzer division was hidden in its ruins, Allied patrols opened fire on carefully reconstructed Pompeii; its buildings were again demolished.

Alkest,
Property of M. Valerius Aurus; and Nicolas Flamel

       Sun, moon: the watch changes. Working
       this week the Villa foundry, I borrow
       lead while the guard shifts, a piece
       in my cheek, one wedged under bracelet, one
       thumb-sized, a piece pea-sized, snuck
       each day out into the world
       for the glory of our Lord the Messiah
       Jesus the Jew. Would He condone this
       theft? But He understood the criminal
       sleight, how I choose to be Christ's
       servant but no senator's slave, how
       once my hands on the auction-block soured
       like bad wine in the shackles' metal press
       so bad that for days they cupped the stink of that
       moment's confinement and now delight
       in the thief's dextrous ten-step finger-dance.
       And this He would comprehend better
       than the crime it is to speak His name
       or secretly scribe it in this scroll

In my dream, an angel appeared to me and held before me a
magnificent book of antique script. 'Flamel, look at this book.
You will not in the least understand it, neither will anyone
else; but a day will come when you will see in it something
that no one else will see.' On a propitious day in 1357, walking
the waking world, I found that same tome in a vendor's stall!
Written in gold on its title page: 'The Jew Abraham, Prince,
Priest, Levite, Astrologer, and Philosopher. The Jewish people
the wrath of God dispersed among the Gauls, greetings and
blessing.' Perhaps it was taken from the poor Jews or found in
one of their abandoned houses.

       rolled safe away from eyes' pry. Untie
       this diary-roll for any centurion's patrolling peer-
       into-slave-quarters: fwik! fwik! the lash

for Alkest's back. But Apostle Paul
when he spoke among the African marble
porticoes of Pozzouli almost sixty years
after the death of Our Lord on Earth
—I was six, and fetching a Naples censer home—
told His hands held leper hands
and whore breasts and slave faces
tight, in unguent. I think His
carpenter-hands would salute my own
deft fingering. That day, returning
home to Pompeii south through the Sea Gate,
my child-eyes shone like stars above
the birth of something holy in me.
We, too, trial; completing the first Horse,
six of us furtive in the abandoned attic:
at the sound of cuirass rattling downstairs
we hushed, our own flesh hung crucified

On the second page the author comforted his people in exile
and exhorted them to avoid vice and idolatry and await the
coming of the Messiah in quiet patience. Starting with page
three, he describes in simple words how metals may be changed.
He probably wanted to help the Jewish people in captivity to
pay their taxes to the Roman emperors. Most of the symbolism
I could not understand—the winged Mercury, the griffons, the
rose-tree, and the rest—and decided to hide the book from the
world's eyes, much as the use of such symbols implied should
be done, and assure that the secret not be used for base ends.

on its row of spines and clavicles;
but the centurions passed our loft. Last week,
that. Now the bronze beast completed,
and left is only the lead trim for fringe and bells
I bring to consecrate our equine icon
from coffers and bins made better
by such stealthy contribution; call it
thieving. Or call it charity. We would
feed all begging freedmen if we could, a coin
on every desperate tambourine, had we one

111

coin-pouch between us. But Christ
the child, the charitable, Jesus the Lamb
would be too obvious and out
of place gracing a Forum; Christ the Lion
rearing among the marketstalls at his foes
from a metal pedestal—too daring a move;
yet this: a common martial statuary,
a horse! donated by anonymous names
to focus all eyes in the Forum, while to us the steed
is secret sign of Christ the Bearer of Suffering
on His Back, Christ the Conveyor, Jesus

For twenty-one years I labored over the illustrations therein,
as I deemed correct by the book's twenty-one pages, and yet
my progress was scant. The picture I copied and hung upon the
charnel house was: the destruction of the Bethlehem infants
under Herod's orders; the spilled blood was caught by the soldiers and poured into a large vessel in which the sun and the
moon seemed to bathe. And yet this public display of the picture brought no enlightened inquiry to my door. I resolved
that since a book written by Abraham the Jew for the Jewish
race would be understood only by a Jewish scholar, I would
pilgrimage to Spain to find just such a Cabbalist.

as Horse; and our Lord in His guise praised
by all Roman passers-by! No, no, do a whole four-
horsed quadriga! suggests Abinnericus, Jew
made moneyed by wine-trade, and finances us.
And so, the first Horse completed, and the second's
pieces scattering the attic floor in preparation.
Those fat silver satyrs and river-nymphs
I beat into decoration for Master's atrium,
gross little figurines! But this Bronze Bearer,
yes, to help mold metal nostrils neighing
as audible as breath from true flesh, yes,
to cast the chest yet quivering its warm ores
to my eyes, to so play with silhouette-line
and life! at once, is fit way to spend those days
Master lounges on the loggia of the sanatorium

away at Stibae, or nights: dream
parades of horses, herds, crosses glinting in eyes
and women borne on their backs. Why not,
sweet Christ Conveyor, carry love

The book itself, too precious to expose to the dangers of the
journey, I left with my loving and pious Pernelle. In 1378 I
donned palmer's gown, took staff and cockleshell, and set off.
For a full year I searched the synagogues in vain. In León on
the way home the answer to my prayers to Saint James, saint
of the occult, met me in the form of Maitre Canches, physician
of Jewish antecedents and Christian faith, most learned man.
We left through Oviedo and Sanson, then up the Loire as far
as Orleans. There my dear Maitre Canches died after sea-fever;
after sharing his knowledge. I returned home alone.

to us? I think, as I carry myself this night
to the low-lit *lupanar*, to the House of Love.
No skulking through the colonnades for a slave
disguised as freedman, else his stealth itself
is suspect! Then: whistle, if you will, walk loud!
Past true freedmen, peddlers hawking pilfered
sweet-meats; past the night's street-clowns
tapping wood clappers; past the blessed Bakery
where one of us, Tinar Property of Eronius the Bread-Man,
sneaks our raw bronze nuggets through
corn-mill and oven, into the kneading-room to hide
our once-weekly night's work in loaves of dough;
and down past the Street of Mercury where my Myrtle
works her ass into any position for one dull *as*
clinking in her cup—and yet is chaste, her love
making bought by any bidder, but love itself
saved for Alkest the Slave. Was not Venus, sacred
goddess of this city herself, clad about her blushing
breasts and maiden-mound by the virgin
myrtle leaves, when first she stepped to earth?
And so tonight I write on the wall 'Good day.
I am as full as a wine-skin. Myrtle,
may your sneeze bring you luck!' and sign

113

With the new-found knowledge I arrived. Pernelle alone aided me, faithful wife, who meditated with me about God and devoted herself to charitable works. In her presence alone, the five-and-twentieth day of April following, in the same year 1382, about five o'clock in the evening, I took the lead that had been turned to silver purer than the silver of mines, and mixed it in the Elixir. And with this I made projection of the Red Stone upon half a pound of mercury; which I transmuted truly into about the same quantity of pure gold.

> *Alkest suspirium puellarum,* 'answer
> to a maiden's prayer.' Ha! and here, with her,
> her favorite position done up in red-and-gold
> above her cubicle and the door barred to sight,
> a huge amphora of wine made mull with honey
> at hand, her necklace against my bare chest
> till like a cardium pot I am shell-impressed
> with her distinctive design, on this night:
> as I raise my own man's monument to her
> and my offering accepted, my brain
> apart from my heart contemplates the concept
> of giving, the joy of the gift, and the monument
> soon to be raised by the city to Jesus Our True King
> Come to Mankind. And kneeling to Myrtle's
> cunt or she to my cock, is not this kneeling
> under the gaze of God as surely as any other
> prayer to Him? as surely as bowing before Him
> Who hangs on the wood cross in our hidden loft?
> Vesuvius, she rumbled all week and continues; yes
> in boyhood I once saw her own molten gold,
> as I pray my lead-and-bronze may, re-mix and rise

I had indeed enough when I had once done it, but I found exceeding great pleasure and delight in seeing and contemplating the admirable works of Nature. In all, five projections I made, and with these grant gold where it will do most good, the churches, the hospitals, and I leave our servants well-provided-for at my death, as they have been kindly treated in life. The grace of God blessed my work and my thousand bungling

trials. The blood of the innocent children was the spirit of
the metals. For my thanks at the joy of reviving such, let the
visitor look at Pernelle and me painted on the chapel door at
the feet of Saint James of the Mystic Arts.

shining from the dead, in new form.

Note: Alkest (54-79), a Pompeiian slave, is a character of my own invention; equally as
invented is the plot of a secret conclave of Christian slaves to donate an anonymously cast
statue of Christ-as-Horse to the Pompeii Forum. But many of the names and details of
the story are true to the Pompeii-Herculaneum excavations. A secret chapel, with an
early cross symbol, was discovered. And a great bronze horse was excavated during
Winckelmann's sojourn. "Restored" by the inexpert Joseph Canart, many of its unearthed
pieces were melted down and reappeared as figures of saints and candelabra for the royal
chapel. Nicolas Flamel (1330-1417) was a goodly French scrivener-turned-alchemist who
dedicated his life to a difficult quest for the culmination of the Art—in conjunction with
the ancient idea of the alchemist's soul being purified in the process of changing base
metal to gold. With his life's supply of this converted metal, Flamel provided for the
foundation-endowment of fourteen hospitals, three chapels, and seven churches in Paris,
and for similar benefactions at Boulogne and Pontoise. His story as here recorded is
reworded primarily from *Alchemy* by E.J. Holmyard.

Village Wizard
1300

Begged by a novice-wizard to display the secret
of his craft, Waziri demonstratively
kept silent.

Asked to perform at the Merchants Bazaar
a feat never seen before, Waziri came
with a dozen coins in his purse and left
with a dozen coins in his purse.

Requested by the husbandless maid to conjure,
Waziri concocted three gifts: a flask of lotion
scented with spice; a beaker of potion
made with grapes; and a potent amulet
wrought with pearl to wear on a necklace
between her breasts when she bared her breasts
to the waxing moon. Even her husband
called it magic.

Paid to recite a spell for sleep, Waziri
began his life story.

Told to foresee the Emperor's future,
Waziri closed his eyes.

Ordered to exorcise evil influence
from the royal heir at his birth,
Waziri cut the umbilical cord.

Commanded on pain of death to provide the impossible
virgin speculum for the Queen, that fabled mage's mirror
so pure, it would have imaged nothing—not its maker,
not the air, and not the darkness—before her face
reflected there: with pity's stare, Waziri, wizard,
wept that tear.

The Harem Boy
1400

Thirty thousand children marched to join the Crusades and recapture Christ's
sepulcher. Asked where they were going, they answered: "To God." Two treacherous
shipowners took them to Alexandria, where they sold the children to the Saracen leaders
and to slave dealers.

— based on Mircea Eliade's account

When I'm good, God allows me to pomade his buttocks.
When I'm bad, it's the straps; or maybe the lit candle
sconced in my own hole. But mostly I tend
to God's potted fronds, and the viziers — their
respective thirsts. God's name is al
Hakkim, and God rides six cream-colored stallions.

*

When the ship docked, I'd bounced like unroped cargo.
I'd wanted to end in a cloud. Instead: this marble
alcove. The days pass by ones, like military inspection.
I know there's a God my God-of-the-Stallions-and-Salves is
mortal for — the God who's Jesus and Mary. But breath's a
cloud too; and viziers' kisses make my only real weather.

*

Once, I thought I'd reach Jesus through Space — one
step, another step, over Europe. Now I understand
Time. The fronds wake up thirsty — one day, another day.
Sometimes, when I take him in my mouth
soft as rosin and harden him, he floats so gently I
hum the Our Father. One service; many prayed to.

Puritania

1600

Sparrows were falling. On every one
God's eye, that peacock feather, was pasted.
Today was the day to strop the blades.
There were four seasons; winter,
like winter water, was hard. The first snows
hit like brass studs. One day The Tempter
was in the leek patch, but fire
applied to the tongue of the maid who saw him
drove him out. Melissa Prentiss
had a voice like unto a nightingale.
They smiled, and sang. They could not put
their hands in their pockets. God's eye
was pasted on everyone. Today
was the day to tan the hides. The Deceiver
was seen in the hog trough. Today
was the day to grind the ax. The buckle
functioned, and kept them in. They worked.
Their jewelry was a night
in the stocks. They wore black,
and black. The first snows and God's eye
were black. The buckle framed the prong.
Today was the day to strap the wife
and carve the poultry. The first snows
cut, like saws. God's paste
was cold. One day The Devil's eye
was long, and icy, upon her
in bed. It was hard.
They walked to Los Angeles.
It was hard. They bundled,
and bundled up.

"On the outskirts of London he recognized angels walking among the haymakers."

—D.V. Erdman, on Blake

The pondtop, gone oily, takes all seven
faces of light. A part of that prismy surface
rises—dragonfly wings—arches and settles

a moment at the grainfields: such a great store
of gold for the foot of such a small rainbow! Later, the
gleaners bend for grain like a bird's peck

slowed and expanded in human function.
Each is a loneliness, carries a loneliness
as a jar does: round, interior

potential. From far, their backs are a piano's
hammers, the disparate striking, the
one song. The youngest, the miller's boy, runs

circles so fast he blurs—they can see the gold
world through him. This makes the translucent
skirts of an angel an angel lives inside.

**"In 1856 she won second prize in the Bread Division
at the local Cattle Show..."**

—Ellmann & O'Clair

The poultry pecks its cages like nightmare
clockworks. They're the universe,
maybe, before man thinks up Sequential Time.
Their skins are a first dream of quill pens. And

so the undulant fields about her today,
light wheats, and brooding ryes, are raw
tables: schema of home and safety. This
is a County Fair, and here's a choir of strawberry jams

beneath their paraffin halos, and these
are the showcattle being rubbed between
brushed flanks so in pleasure they'll
still for the judges ... She looks down.

A bee is architecting
air around a flower. The judges are here.
The bee see the bee see the bee. And now
they've left, with ahems. And now she's writing

We know, by now—the Word was first
And—after—earth, and grain, and grass—
As world to Him—'tis rising, now,
The making of my Second Place.

"and in the preface declared, 'So far as I am aware,
I happen to be the only English poet who has brought out
a new volume of verse on his   birthday...'
He meant to write in 'eighty-eighth,' but did not quite
make it: the volume appeared after his death on January 11."
                                        —Ellmann & O'Clair

Outside it purpled
then grayed. The book was *Winter Words*,
the ink was cold and black.
He thought of darkling thrushes,
rising from the inkwell, clearing the sill.
And then he didn't remember.

The snow fell.
He looked at that blank
white space it made on the ledge,
and heard the sky say Now,
so late, what a shame it would be
for even one word to disturb it.

His Daughter

the spelling etc. modernized

Last night his puling
angels again!—Gave me but two hours' sleep and
then that sweet black cream was skimmed.
So to his rooms. He looks like a cheese
in the tapers. The angels work his tongue
like a maggot dancing in cheese.
Oh his wee-winged angels! Just writing
this, now, the quill makes me to vomit.

*

Must read at him French, must read at him Greek...
Well he is a fribbling bufflehead and ninny!
In the market we contrived to let go
his hand, and oh it was sweet as sillabub, so
to see him lurch about the pickling tubs
and ruddle-dip vats! It ended on his breeches-seat
at a cart of Greek olives and French wines which
he was blind to as much as their language.

*

Out the window, a dog-sled belled like a silver
aviary competes with the somber iron sound of St. Giles's.
Sometimes the sun through the trees is a perfect gold hair's-comb.
Out the window...trained parrots and lilac-water!
On the green the girls wear satin,
Fix their flounces, flirt, and fatten;
Here, it's chill, severe, and Latin.
—You see, I am his daughter.

*

Mr. Marvell is cherry-cheeked. He said it was not *moos*
but *muse*, but kindly, though under the quilt Old

122

Sour Scrunch-Face greened like a LEEK PIE at this news; then
I slipped out. Sometimes no visitors try
the brass knocker all week, and then he is in a lull, and I do
feel sorrow: trapped in his own dark skull like me
in his writing chamber. At least I have a candle! I have drawn
stiff antlers from all his wings today, said Mr. Marvell.

*

"Was I to have never parted from thy side?" So
she is my favorite. Sometimes I feel still a portion
rib—white; hard; attached by a gristle. A pity
the more, that she will deliver a buzzgossip
sermon as readily as any in his world! A SNAKE will busy
my hand with discourse past an hour! I should have hastened
the fruit on our small oak apple-tray, had it meant
an end. But even as they CHEWED they kept atalking.

*

Of a sudden we did picnic today, the wicker overflowing
cold collops, butter peas, muskmelons, and a
pigeon. He was in cheer, with chides and smiles, attending
our tresses with Mama's own Venice red brush.
The wine was white; and in a certain sun, my goblet looked to
be heavy with pure light.—So I drank it not, in a strange toast
to his eyes. A kindness seized me for this patriarch tree
of knowledge, of which I am the most darling pippin!

*

It is a sin to dissemble and yet with Anne I did
this second time sell over a scuttle full of his books
to the ragpickers. I wish him dead. And this is
surely plucking the one heart he knows, from his body! Now
I shall boast the new bonnet for Church, if it requires
lace at the cuff to match, then that as well.
I have no brother. A maid she is my mother.
I wish him to lay with his Wing Things and smother.

123

*

Tonight when he called dictation, I dawdled
among my tortoise-shell boxes and crystals, then no
longer could delay. He was abed, and in the pointing
of light my entrance admitted, thrashed
his linens; as if another light, inside him, strived
to break into our air. Sharp words I had on my tongue I
kept, again. He was also somebody's, no,
something's, amanuensis.—Bones of glow and he the hand.

"Yet Leaving Here a Name, I Trust,/ That Will Not Perish in the Dust"

The only Southey writings still widely read are a few lyrics . . . and—a piece so widely loved and often retold that it has lost its connection with its author and has acquired the status of an anonymous "fairy tale"—the story of The Three Bears.

—Norton

1.

There's something you want to remember—a line of mine, say, or my name—you want to tug it into the light from its old ooze. And maybe your day is filled with the usual begs for attention: the idle encoded teeth of a musicbox, with a pet monkey kilned on its porcelain lid; the burgundy sherbets; that civilized sexual moan from your bed of the kind that supports small flutterings of *yesss* and *pleassse* on its sides, like delicate parasol-fungi enhancing a huge, brute log . . . but you keep on tugging, that something. A convolution, a hook, in your brain wants that fish. So your hip-boots, your wickerwork creel, your cast and cast again . . . Forget it. The line snaps, the bait goes mush, there *are* those bottom-grub-bing things that will never see light, there *is* what's lost, and that's that.

And there is the other sort. That you don't want, that you iced over once and hoped it stayed a fossil, that you never knew exist-ed, that wasn't anywhere in your schedule or inclinations, it is no part of this day's spiralling of lilac sachet or the flutist's tirade from the garden. But, still, no matter the insistence of ivy in ara-besques up the bower's limestone walls; of sherry glazing this gob-let; or sunbonnet making that lady's face a study in amorous shadow . . . there bursts, from the sweatkept underparts of you, a swipe of paw, and in it the rich stink of fin and salt entrails, that says: there's another way of fishing, beneath speech or number, it was here all along.

It was hibernating.

It wakes, you

125

2.
wake   again in the house
of confusion. Every morning, the eyes fight for reassembling
sherd and lopsided plane into what we
call a day, and the hands' corresponding
inner grasps sift mind for a hard, glinting
orientation. This is that
rousing confounded, the memory

> *-lost*
> *-in woods interweaved past admission of sun*
> *-hunger / an open mouth in the belly*
> *-fatigue / a snapped neck in each knee—then*
> > *a clearing*
> *-away of the bloodshot stare's red brambles—& the cottage*
> *-the cottage at noon like a muffin*
> *-the cottage with tulip with ladybeetle with breeze*
> *-with chair / the first of the folkloric threes*
> *-the line between "loneliness" and "solitude" shimmies*
> *-with porridge / its steam a long sweet sausage*
> *-the sentry between "mine" and "notmine" sleeps too*
> *-with bed / with one white dollop of pillow then sleep then wake*

lost in the face of exigency: a looking
at you naked, from those six accusatory
buttony eyes. Fear requires no history; and
having forgotten the rest, this
you will remember as you leap from the window, as
the window catches
the moment like cel on a filmstrip,
this: baby
bear's smile the delicate bone horizon of
Japanese miniature.
                       He is your own
life where it's black at the back of your nostril. Then
you land, pale x, on the lawn
and run home to a proper sleeping

3.
and wake from a dream of Coleridge
Wordsworth & Ch Lamb at a great oak table set
on the knoll like an animal all-fours. They were to
ale and cheddar wedge, and I approached hailing
the three by name, and with endearments, and wanting nothing
so much as my own plate in their company—for clearly
some festive occasion was at hand and even sober
Wm flaunted peeks of crimson in his attire. But
C. said "Who is this
Nonsequitur in our otherwise Smooth Grouping" or
similar query (maybe Anachronism) and I could see
by the pouchy cheek and crag-brow of his
ursine face going edged and contradictory, that he
truly knew me not, and spoke for them,
all. Down near Bristol, the wheels of the mail coach, made
tiny by distance, turned like a clockworks; then
grew smaller; finally, the horses dragged them silently
into disappearance. Then was I surely
sorehearted to tears, which I let
without shame in front of these three true fellows of mine but
they only dandled their mugs as if waiting
a servant to leave. And in this vision I
ran, more stumbled, then rolled, downhill
to the lake, and entered like insignificant
sight in an eye, where I sank to the bottom muckings and
dissolved, there were gnawbones only left now, and people
would drink of this water delighting in its textures and
say This nameless flavor, no, This
natural flavor is so ancient so unforgettable here
my child take your sip.
                         I wrote
it down, by a fresh moon's wanlight, before sun
diverted my focus to the fashionable
louis quinze and porcelains weighting the room—and every
so often halted, to see my name on the page
and my hand (yes a fossil in its flesh, a quill in its palm)
were not yet haze—which as you know is the
premonition and fate of a waking dream. I wrote:

127

4.
Shorten the life of a shine and it's a flash.
There are caves, there are long-remembered
darks in which the slowing of heart to a fitful smoulder means it
survives. The gill the crawlstump the paw's black pad...
I gave such steady light, once...There is this
gold hair twinkling like signals, there are these
beastmarks I best remember myself by.

The Well

a poem about Edward Hicks, with a quote about Millet

1. "... that this scene was what was visible in front of the house where
   Millet was born, and that consciously or unconsciously the artist
   had enlarged the proportions of the well by two thirds so that they
   coincided with his childhood perception."

   —John Berger

One hundred *Peaceable Kingdoms*, and in all of them
the presence of lamb. One hundred tranquil
presences of lamb, its wool in stately curls
like the fresh white shavings of pine. A wolf
will nuzzle it. A wolf and a lamb,
a yang and a yin, will be one simple design.
A cow will knowingly rest the great weight
of her head on the lion's
acquiescent back, no stranger than any
marriage you know. And they have a child.
They have one hundred children,
who yoke them together or hold a flowering branch,
a simple moon face and its simple, dark, plum eyes.
These animals belong together not only
with a puzzle's pieces' beautiful, flush
fit, but with their flatness—Hicks
had painted tavern signs for a living.
These animals pose. These animals say themselves
like any weather vane's beast: become
domesticated, heraldic, and all of them heading
one hundred times in the one direction, the future,
a sweet and peaceful wind blows.

2.   *"The main explanation for Hicks's obsession with the subject must*
     lie with Hicks himself. He was a man distraught, overwhelmed by
     his sense of guilt and unworthiness..."
                                                —Abraham A. Davidson

The dragon smoked like a thwarted desire
—Good! I leaned the ladder over and fired
his breath from my tin of dyer's yellow. Now
half of *The Dragon and Calf* was done—and only
yesterday, in rough, he'd smoked like a
burnt roast: so, my hand has brought ferocity out
of the common. It was night; and my own
throat on fire. Tired, you lose a grip. And I
was tired: all afternoon, in labor over what
the plains of my first three peaceable
kingdoms required, that didn't seem
complete yet; and now this, at the roofedge,
over a room of guzzle and guffaw...and
women. The night was a purple, the window a
torch-orange wash. The grip I lost was something
in me; my grip on the ladder was never
more sure. Her hair was wild like the thatch
that brushed my cheek, it might have had a
roofthatch's insect life in it, surely it smelt
of the purple night wind...And two men
walking their hands on her bodice's muslin,
that I from my rung could look
down fully to the nipples' pink meat...
My throat on fire; and rubbing against the ladder
until it broke, or until I broke...then on
the ground, a ruffian ruckus behind me, and
then running home. And then home. And then
washing it off these hands, the whole
paint-purple-pinkness of it, rinsing the least
pink weakness off, and drinking
deep from the cool kitchen pitcher where
pewter gives water an extra heft, recognizing
the power it takes to cleanse. And then
I knew. In one I did the Delaware River, just

a pure rush over rock, I did it
completely before I slept, and sketched a laving
line of water in the other two—they said yes,
this is it. This is the place where a boy can breathe
air in and out like the white
flag of peace, at a brookside, being laundered.

3. *"His* Residence of David Twining, 1787 . . . *is a nostalgic recreation of a yearned-for peaceful childhood . . ."*

—Abraham A. Davidson

The land goes up three-fourths of the canvas
and so, by perspective, we understand
the vastness of childhood's holdings, and
how this is a well-farmed firm-built world
against a strip of sky that must
define itself in terms of human doing. The doing
is good: a worker plows an even patch in furrows
regular as a ledger's lines; his light horse
and his dark horse move in synchrony like a light horse
and its well-packed shadow cast standing
up on the air. Four hogs in pleasingly
decreasing size, like a musical scales. A cat's arched back
like an architect's stencil. Everywhere: poise,
prosperity in a sane amount. In front, the good Quaker
David Twining opens a pen (a bull and a milk-cow
coo like the stylized doves of a needlepoint), carrying
a bucket: full or empty, we can't tell. Elizabeth
Twining sits with an open Bible. And at her side,
her foster son Edward—down in the canvas's
lower-right corner, his open face: almost the
punctuation ending this well-wrought
sentence of a scene. The doing is *very* good.
And if we understand by perspective, some
understanding is lovely and strange: far back,
for instance, a pump is placed. I'd like to say,
Millet in mind, a well. It isn't quite, it's a pump,
and requires a Quaker's just labor. For its distance
it seems large—a full-grown cow and mare
nearby use no more room. Perhaps
David Twining with his bucket is on his way there
or from there. The pump will wait.
The pump says that there's water, special water,
below this special ground. And when we need it,
when it needs to surface, the pump will be waiting there,
waiting. As large as we need. If we'll only go back.
A hundred times if we need it.